complete jewellery

ASK

 **Reading**
BOROUGH COUNCIL

Reading Borough Libraries

Email: info@readinglibraries.org.uk
Website: www.readinglibraries.org.uk

Reading 0118 9015950
Battle   0118 9015100
Caversham 0118 9015103
Palmer Park 0118 9015106
Southcote 0118 9015109
Tilehurst 0118 9015112
Whitley 0118 9015115

CAV 6/11	04. SEP 15.		
17. AUG 11	19. APR 16.		
22. SEP 11	pat 7/18		
29. MAY 12			
11. OCT 13			
31. JAN 14.			
SOU 9/14			

2009

Author:
Title:

Class no. **745.5942**

To avoid overdue charges please return this book to a
Reading library on or before the last date stamped above.
If not required by another reader, it may be renewed by
personal visit, telephone, post, email, or via our website.

complete jewellery

EASY TECHNIQUES AND 25 GREAT PROJECTS

MARY HELT

COLLINS & BROWN

First published in the United Kingdom in 2009 by
Collins & Brown
10 Southcombe Street
London
W14 0RA

An imprint of Anova Books Company Ltd

Distribution in the United States and Canada by
Sterling Publishing Co, 387 Park Avenue South,
New York, NY 10016-8810, USA

ISBN 978-1-84340-459-0

A CIP catalogue for this book is available from the
British Library.

10 9 8 7 6 5 4 3 2 1

Reproduction by Rival Colour Ltd
Printed and bound by in China by
1010 Printing International Ltd

This book can be ordered direct from the publisher.
Contact the marketing department, but try your
bookshop first.

www.anovabooks.com

contents

introduction

Exploring my mother's jewellery drawer is one of my favourite childhood memories. I discovered earrings made from mini plastic rum bottles, an exquisite carved ivory necklace and souvenir bracelets carried back from across the globe. This was the beginning of a lifelong fascination with all jewellery, from the lowliest plastic charm purchased for a dime, to enormous rocks on display in the world's most important collections.

The art and craft of jewellery making is vast, far greater than any one volume could explain. For the purpose of this book, I've focused on what can be done at home, to wear tomorrow. I've chosen techniques that are easy to learn and adaptable to your own design ideas and favourite materials. These techniques are basic, and widely used in contemporary jewellery design. You don't need loads of special equipment, only some select tools to begin with, and a few others for the advanced techniques at the end of the book. After that, if you have found techniques that have ignited your passion, there are many more books to read, and classes to take, on all sorts of methods.

Each chapter introduces the basic techniques that you require, followed by a selection of projects to put everything into practice. The first chapter is devoted to stringing. Stringing is elemental to jewellery making and you'll find that the tools used here will be useful in all sorts of other jewellery-making applications. In the Wire Wrapping chapter, a favourite of mine, you'll learn how to form wire with all sorts of specialised pliers that will be the envy of your household. Next, I'll show you the delights of Polymer Clay, and touch on the sculptural versatility this material offers. In the Textiles chapter, we'll work on some nifty projects from fabrics, such as wool felt and lightweight printed cotton. In the Advanced Techniques chapter, we'll go a little further with wire wrapping and stringing techniques, along with an introduction to making your own simple jewellery findings with a kitchen torch and a jeweller's hammer.

I hope to provide you with a foundation of simple techniques and ideas for a jewellery wardrobe bursting with your own creations. Some of the techniques are simple, and some will require a bit of practice. Don't be discouraged if you don't immediately make things perfectly; I still have to practise and make mistakes to learn, too. Even if you focus on just one or two methods, you'll be able to make many pieces of jewellery to wear, and even give as gifts. Have fun creating, and I hope you enjoy the book.

tools & materials

Before you make a start on any of the projects, you will
need to gather together the essential tools and materials.
While there are several pieces of equipment that provide a
basic foundation for any jewellery making, each technique
calls for more specialist tools. I have listed those that I find
essential and given you a brief guide to what is available
in the craft stores to make your life easier.

basic equipment

These pieces of equipment should be kept in your basic crafting box, close to hand, ready to be called upon whatever project you are creating.

Beading awl – Used to form and tighten knots in the beading thread, this is one of my favourite tools. I have an all-metal one, but they are also available with a wooden handle. It has many other uses, such as piercing holes in polymer clay and is handy for making holes in cardstock, in case you end up selling some earrings and need a quick packaging item.

Craft knife and cutting mat – A sharp knife is often called upon and the cutting mat will protect your work surface and provide a level surface to work on.

Crimp beads – Used at the end of the strands of beading wire to secure the loop that holds the clasp or jump ring at the end of the wire securing your beads. These are barrel-shaped beads that come in base metal, although I recommend using sterling silver or gold-filled barrel-shaped crimps for best results.

Crimping pliers – Used to compress the crimp bead against the wire. A set of crimping pliers has two notches on the jaw, a mouth-shaped notch to make the initial crimp and an O-shaped notch that rounds out the bead to make a nicely shaped, secure ending.

Jewellery pliers – A basic set of jewellery pliers includes chain-nose pliers, round-nose pliers and flat-nose pliers. Invest in the best quality pliers you can afford as less expensive pliers tend to lose alignment much more quickly than higher quality pliers.

Jewellery wire cutters – Used to snip the ends of the beaded strand when you are finished.

Scissors – An essential item! I like to use embroidery scissors to cut thread, as well as sharp wire cutters. Specialised thread-cutting scissors are available. Keep a pair for cutting paper and a separate pair for cutting fabric and thread.

Tape measure and ruler – Accurate measuring is essential when cutting lengths of wire or thread.

Tweezers or needle-nose pliers – A useful piece of equipment. Can be used for undoing knots or in place of an awl when making knots.

Safety First

• Always wear eye protection when cutting wire or using a torch for soldering.

• Wear an apron when using a torch, or working with chemicals or polymer clay.

• Follow the manufacturer's safety instructions when using a torch.

• Wash your hands thoroughly after handling polymer clay or chemicals.

• Keep your eyes on your work when hammering or using sharp tools such as felting needles – watch your fingers!

❶ Tools for Stringing

Awl – See page 10. An awl is useful if your end loop slips and becomes too small before you crimp your crimp bead. Use the tip of the awl to re-open the loop.

Bead board – Made out of inexpensive flocked plastic, this is useful when laying out beads for a design. Bead boards come with grooves to arrange single and multiple strands. They also have wells to store beads and findings.

Bead mat – A mat is useful when beading to prevent the beads from rolling around your work surface. I also use them when doing a knotting project. Alternatively, a hand towel works well.

Beading thread – For classic bead stringing. Available in a wide variety of sizes and colours on cards, with a pre-attached wire needle, and spools in silk and nylon. I tend to use the spools as they are more economical, and if I make a mistake, I don't feel like it is such a waste! Silk and nylon beading thread are lovely beading materials, especially for necklaces and bracelets. They are both found in similar colour ranges, and similar diameters, ranging from very fine, such as Size 00 (0.13mm), to thick, such as Size FFF (0.42mm). I use Gudebrod® silk for pearls and stones in Size D or E. Silk thread is primarily used in knotting pearls and gemstone beads (see pages 140–143). It has a beautiful texture, and gives a wonderful drape. Nylon can be used for many applications, and is preferable to silk when the beads are heavy, or have bigger holes, since you can find a better colour range in the larger diameters when the wire may be visible. I use C-Lon Micro in a diameter of 0.12mm.

Crimp beads – See page 10. Used at the end of the strands of beading wire to secure the loop that holds the clasp or jump ring.

Crimping pliers – See page 10. Used to compress the crimp bead against the wire.

Flexible beading wire – A fine, nylon-coated cable that is used with crimp beads for stringing all sorts of items. Tigertail is the predecessor to modern flexible beading wire, and is thicker and more likely to kink. Manufacturers such as Soft Flex® and Beadalon® have introduced flexible beading wire that is fine and supple. The most basic flexible beading wire is grey in colour, but a variety of colours, as well as silver and gold plate, are also available, along with fine, medium and heavy gauges. The diameter of the wire varies with manufacturer, but I tend to use fine and medium gauge. Fine is great for pearls and semi-precious stone beads with small holes. Medium is used for Czech glass beads and larger stone beads.

G-S Hypo Cement – This is a type of strong glue, used here on knots for added strength.

Twisted wire needles – There are different types of beading needles, but I use a twisted wire needle to string beads. Twisted wire needles come in different sizes, 6, 8 and 10 being the most common. I tend to use Size 8 for most projects and Size 10 if the holes of the beads are large enough, since the wire is thicker and less likely to bend. If the bead holes are very small, which is sometimes the case with pearls or small gemstone beads, a Size 6 needle is best.

❷ Tools for Wire Wrapping

Head pins – Pieces of wire that have either a ball on one end, or a flat 'head'. Used to hold a bead and create a dangle when used with a wire-wrapped loop.

Jeweller's flannel polishing cloth – Used to shine your piece after you have finished.

Needle files – These can be used to file away and smooth any rough ends of the wire after you've cut it.

Pliers – See also page 10. When I make wire wrapped jewellery, I use the following pliers: chain-nose pliers, bent-nose pliers and round-nose pliers. Chain-nose pliers have a flat inner nose and a rounded outer nose. Bent chain-nose pliers are the same, except that the nose is bent. They may be a little harder to find, but they are great for wire wrapping and also for opening and closing jump rings. Round-nose pliers are used to make the round loops you'll need in making a wire-wrapped bead.

Ring mandrel – A steel mandrel engraved with different ring sizes is very useful when making wire rings.

Sterling silver wire – This is a favourite among wire wrappers, since it is malleable and can be bent several times before breaking. It has a prettier glow than silver-coated craft wire or nickel and is much more expensive. Sterling silver wire comes in a few different tempers, or hardnesses. Dead soft is a very soft temper, which is useful when you are first learning to wire wrap. As you manipulate the wire, it begins to harden on its own, and I have found that when wire wrapping with a large enough gauge, the wire-wrapped loops of soft tempered silver are hard enough for most purposes. Half-hard is the next temper, and is widely used in wire wrapping. It requires a little firmer torque when you are making a loop, but makes nice, firm loops. Hard and extra hard sterling wire are great with 20 gauge wire to make ear wires.

Wire – Craft wire is usually made from copper, with a coloured coating. You can use this for many projects, and for practising techniques before using silver wire. Uncoated copper wire is great for practising wire wrapping techniques. Nickel silver, also called German silver, is a mix of copper, zinc and nickel.

Wire cutters – Also called flush cutters, these are used to cut the wire and trim any excess.

Gauge Guide

Wire is found in several gauges, or widths, and all kinds of metals. There are a few units of measurement used in the jewellery industry. I have used the B&S wire gauge units. For wire wrapping very small holes found in small gemstone beads or pearls, I use 26 gauge wire, or 24 gauge wire if the holes will allow it. For wrapping glass beads and larger gemstone beads, I use 24 or 22 gauge. When making a ring, 18 or 16 gauge wire works well. Below I have listed a guide to the equivalent diameters in mm and inches for a selection of gauges.

B&S Gauge	mm	inches
0	8.26	0.325
5	4.61	0.182
10	2.57	0.101
12	2.05	0.081
14	1.63	0.064
16	1.29	0.051
18	1.02	0.04
20	0.81	0.032
22	0.64	0.025
24	0.51	0.02
26	0.41	0.016
28	0.33	0.013
30	0.25	0.01

Acrylic rolling pin – A good basic for rolling out the clay. A straight-sided drinking glass can be used as an alternative if you can't find an acrylic rolling pin.

Alcohol – Use a cloth dampened with alcohol to remove dust from your work surface and rolling pin, and to eliminate tackiness.

Awl, stylus or toothpick – See page 10. The awl is a versatile implement for clay work. You can use it to piece holes to make pendants, and to give textures to clay surfaces.

Baking sheet – After you have finished shaping and decorating your piece, you'll need to bake it. Use a baking sheet, with parchment paper underneath the clay item.

Clay cutters, cookie and fondant cutters – These die-cut cutters are made from metal or plastic, and come in a variety of shapes and sizes. Some craft stores and polymer clay websites have cutters available specifically for polymer clay. A cake decorating supply shop may also have a good variety of cutters you can use for clay. Ones made for cutting rolled fondant come in small sizes, which are perfect for cutting jewellery-sized pieces of clay.

Craft knife – You'll need a sharp xacto knife for most polymer clay projects.

Cutting mat and parchment paper – For my work surface, I use a flexible, self-healing cutting mat with a piece of parchment paper taped to it with strong tape. After you work on a polymer project, you can cut the piece of parchment paper surrounding the polymer so you don't have to directly touch it en route to the oven.

Glossy finishing glaze and small paintbrush – After a polymer piece is baked, you can leave the surface or you can coat it with a glaze for shininess. Use a small paintbrush, and apply 2–4 coats. There are glazes made specifically for polymer clay, such as Studio by Sculpey, or you can try an acrylic polyurethane.

Long, flexible cutting blade – This looks like an extra-long razor blade. I use it to cut excess clay from the back of my pressed, moulded pieces.

Oven – A regular kitchen oven works best. It is widely thought that fumes from polymer are safe; however, if you have concerns, you can avoid fumes by forming a tent with aluminium foil over your polymer clay object while baking. An alternative is to purchase a toaster oven specifically for polymer clay baking. Experiment with scrap clay before putting a project into the oven.

Oven thermometer – A free-standing oven thermometer is a necessity for baking clay. Even though ovens have a temperature dial, they can be off by several degrees.

Polymer clay – Available in several different varieties and brands, polymer clay is a modelling material that is soft and pliable, until you cure it by baking in the oven. Some brands have a hard consistency, some are softer. The texture after baking will also vary, some have a matt finish, others are a little more glossy. I suggest buying a few packs of different brands and seeing what you like to work with the best.

Ruler – To measure the thickness of the clay when you roll it out.

Wet/dry sandpaper, 400 grit and finer – Use wet sandpaper to smooth any rough edges after baking your item.

Optional tools (but worth it!)

Clay extruder – A clay extruder is a metal tube that forces clay through an interchangeable disc. A selection of discs come with the extruder, which will allow you to make uniform coils of ribbon and tiles, among other shapes. One variety works by using a plunger mechanism. The other type works by using a screw-type twisting action, which is much easier on your hands.

Dremel hand drill – A motorised tool that is very useful in all types of jewellery making, including polymer clay. It is great for buffing with the flannel wheel, and for drilling holes.

❹ Tools for Textiles

Crochet cotton – You can crochet using many different weights and types of yarn, from fineweight to 4-ply and double-knitting yarns. However, I have used a Perle cotton thread (#5) for the crochet projects. It is strong and easier to work with than rayon or silk. The fine gauge works well with the small hook for jewellery projects, and it also has an attractive sheen.

Crochet hooks – Available in metal, plastic and wood, crochet hooks come in a range of sizes to suit your piece. For making the small beads and delicate embellishments in the projects, I have used a Size 1 (2.00mm) steel hook.

Felting needles – Used to pull the wool fleece and separate the fibres to felt the wool. They come in different sizes, Size 36 and 38 are recommended for felting balls. The needles are very sharp, so be extra careful and pay close attention when using them.

Foam felting pad – A high-density small foam block that you place on your work surface to take the impact of the needles as you push them through the wool fibres. It also gives some protection against the needles breaking on a hard surface.

Needle and thread – For sewing by hand.

Sewing machine – For one sewing project I used a sewing machine, which I have had little experience with, but loved the results and am inspired to do more. So, if I can use a sewing machine to sew a straight line with a little guidance from my mom and a little practise on my own, you can, too! If you haven't sewn before, a friend or relative probably has, and it only takes a little time to learn to sew a straight stitch.

Wool tops (roving) – Fluffy wool fleece. I used merino and corriedale wool for the needle felting projects, as these types of wool are quick to felt and have fine fibres that don't result in a lot of fuzziness.

Tools for Advanced Techniques

Bench block – A small square of steel that you use under the hammer when you strike the metal.

Chasing hammer – There is an assortment of jeweller's hammers available, such as ball peen hammers, planishing hammers, rawhide hammers and chasing hammers. For the projects in this book, I've used a chasing hammer. This can be purchased from a jeweller's supply company (see page 156). A chasing hammer is really designed to strike chasing tools to create incised designs in metal. It is a very versatile hammer for the beginner, since it will flatten metal wire with one side, and create a textured hammered surface with the other side.

Copper wire – For practising, as this is soft enough to hammer with desired results, and is much less expensive than silver wire.

Eye protection – While using your hammer and wire, please use eye protection and take extra care as you'll be hammering close to your fingers.

Flux – A solution of boric acid, used here to lessen the firescale created by the torch, which is the black finish you'll see when sterling is heated. Flux is found in liquid and paste form, and is used in soldering to help solder flow. After heating the wire, you can completely remove the firescale by dropping it in a 'pickle' solution. This can be made using a solution of citric acid, found in the home baking section of the supermarket, or alum, found in the spice section.

Gemstone beads – Come in a seemingly endless assortment of colours and grades. There is a wide range in quality of stones available for purchase. You can choose from semi-precious gems, such as garnet, amethyst, chalcedonay, emerald, jade, rose quartz and freshwater pearls. Choose carefully and consider using precious metal findings to do the gems justice.

Gold and platinum wire – Carat gold, although expensive, is the best kind of metal for wire wrapping as it is very malleable and holds loops well, even at fine gauges. Solid gold wire, as opposed to gold-filled or plated wire, is graded by carats. All gold, except for 24 carat gold, is alloyed with silver and copper for strength. A small amount of gold can be purchased to make earrings.

Silver wire – Most of the wire-wrapping projects in this book use silver-coloured wire or sterling wire. Pure silver wire, also called fine silver, is usually too soft to wire wrap with; however, I use it to make head pins for very small gemstone beads as it doesn't firescale when heated, and doesn't need to have a pickle bath. I also use it to make French wire, since it doesn't tarnish and is easier to care for over time.

Small butane torch – A hot enough flame to melt silver. These can be bought from a jewellery supplier and also from kitchen supply stores.

Gemstone Buying Guide

When buying stones from a dealer, look to see if the gemstones are of a uniform size on a strand. Even if the diameter is the same, the height of the bead usually won't be. I try to get strands that are as uniform as possible, although this is not feasible with small beads. Check the faceting and look for beads that have crisp and sharp facets. Holes that are uniform, with smooth edges that won't fray thread, are important, too. A hole that is wide enough for fine wire or thread is obviously important. A reputable gemstone bead dealer will disclose, honestly, if the beads are dyed, heated or are natural. Many stones have been heated to stabilize the colour. Natural stones are the most valuable, and you will pay for them dearly, but it is worth it!

stringing

I consider stringing to be the backbone of jewellery making. It uses easily acquired materials, and can teach a fundamental sense of arranging colours and shapes into a pleasing design. It's also great for learning how to manipulate tiny items with your hands, using tension and angle to achieve different results. The methods are interchangeable in the projects, so if you find that you'd rather use a needle and thread for a project calling for beading wire, go for it!

Stringing with flexible beading wire

This is a simple way to quickly make beaded necklaces, bracelets and even earrings. Few tools are used; only the beading wire, crimp beads and a pair of crimping pliers plus wire cutters are necessary. Since the beading wire is somewhat stiff, beads glide on easily without a needle. You can use all types of beads in this method, from very lightweight pearls on a fine gauge beading wire, to heavy glass beads on a thicker wire.

You will need:

Medium beading wire
Tube- or barrel-shaped seamless crimp
    beads, sterling or gold filled
Crimping pliers
Wire cutters
Beading awl

1 Adding crimp bead

Cut the desired length of beading wire. While holding the wire in one hand about 4cm (1½in) from the end, slide on a crimp bead. Push the short end of the stringing wire back through the bead, creating a loop.

2 Crimping

Adjust the size of the loop by pulling the crimp bead towards it, making it smaller, but large enough to let a jump ring move freely. To start the crimping process, place the crimp bead of the loop you formed in the bow-shaped opening in the pliers, with the hole of the bead facing you. Squeeze the pliers closed firmly to create a crushed crimp bead with a c-shape around the wire.

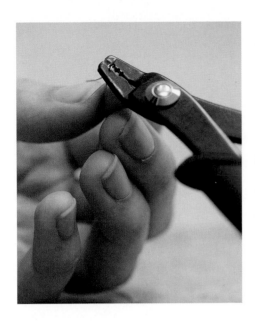

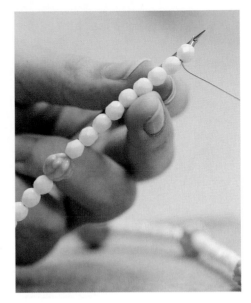

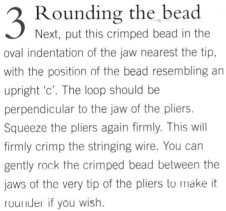

3 Rounding the bead

Next, put this crimped bead in the oval indentation of the jaw nearest the tip, with the position of the bead resembling an upright 'c'. The loop should be perpendicular to the jaw of the pliers. Squeeze the pliers again firmly. This will firmly crimp the stringing wire. You can gently rock the crimped bead between the jaws of the very tip of the pliers to make it rounder if you wish.

4 Adding beads

Slide your first bead onto the strand of stringing wire. Let the tail of the wire from the crimped loop pass through the hole of the bead if the bead hole is big enough. Trim the excess wire and then string on all the beads for the project.

5 Finishing

When you have strung on the last bead, slip on another crimp bead as you did in Step 1, and pull the tail end of the wire through the hole of the crimp bead, and the bead next to it, creating a loop as you did in Step 1. Pull the end of the wire, taking up the slack with the awl, so that the crimp bead rests snugly next to the last bead. Repeat Step 2 to secure the crimp bead. Open the jump ring (see page 25) and attach it to the loop, then slip on the clasp while still holding the jump ring open. Close the jump ring.

Classic bead stringing

Bead stringing with a needle and thread is the method that has been used for hundreds of years. Even though it is more economical than using flexible beading wire, I think it gives a traditional quality finish, especially when using pearls and semi-precious gemstone beads.

You will need:
Flexible beading needle
Silk or nylon thread, such as C-Lon Micro
   0.12mm
Beads and clasp
Jump ring
French wire
Wire cutters
Beading awl
G-S Hypo Cement or strong glue

Stretched to the Limit

Over time, beading thread will stretch, creating unattractive spaces between the beads and the clasp. You can prevent this to an extent by stretching the thread prior to stringing with beads. I recommend stretching the thread overnight by suspending an object weighing 0.5kg (1lb) from the length of thread.

1 Making a slip knot

Thread a beading needle with the required amount of thread, doubling up the thread and closing with a slip knot at the end. Stretch the thread overnight by hanging an object weighing about 0.5kg (1lb) from the loop.

2 First bead

String on one bead and then a jump ring, followed by a section of French wire. Hold the French wire gently as you slide it on, as it will sometimes catch the fibres of the thread and snag.

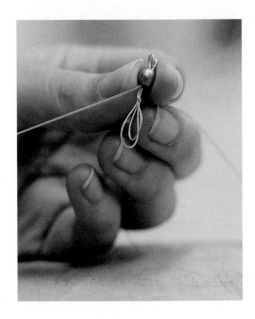

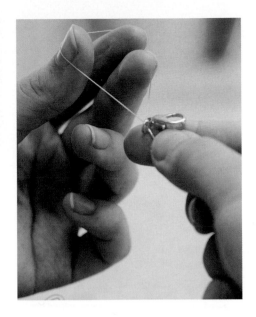

3 French wire loop

Pass the needle attached to the thread back down through the hole of the bead that is closest to the French wire on the adjacent side of the jump ring. Bring the needle out of the bottom hole of the bead next to the slip knot, and pull the thread through gently to form a French wire loop at the top enclosing the jump ring.

4 Stringing

String on the rest of your beads, following a repeated pattern if they are different colours, then slide on a piece of French wire followed by the clasp.

5 Looping the thread

Cut the eye of the needle with wire cutters and remove the needle from the thread. Hold your thumb, forefinger and index finger together, and drape the loop of the thread over them.

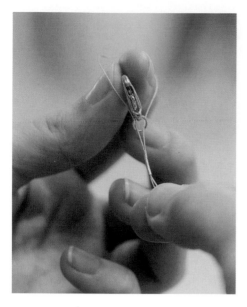

6 Shortening the thread
Pull the French wire with your free hand up towards your fingers. Next, grasp the jump ring, or clasp, with your looped fingers, using your free hand to assist. At the same time, gently pull the strand of thread to pick up the slack with your other hand.

7 Closing the loop
The loop of thread should be to the left of the French wire, and the French wire will take on a backwards 'c' shape. The jump ring should hover over the French wire, as you begin to close the loop by bringing the wire up to shorten it. The loop will get smaller and smaller, until the French wire encases the thread, creating a loop, and the wire contains the jump ring.

8 Tightening the thread
Slide the beads, except for the last two beads, down towards the loop you just made with the French wire. Undo the slip knot. With the thumb and forefinger of one hand, hold on to the loop gently. With the thumb and forefinger of the other hand, pull the tail of the thread, tightening the slack around the point of an awl.

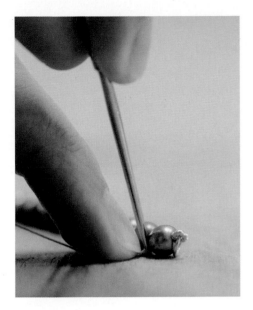

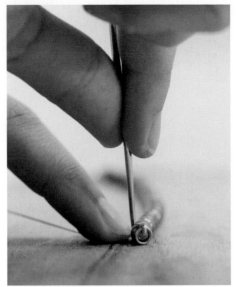

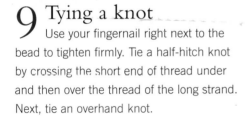

9 Tying a knot

Use your fingernail right next to the bead to tighten firmly. Tie a half-hitch knot by crossing the short end of thread under and then over the thread of the long strand. Next, tie an overhand knot.

10 Finishing

Make a loop with the short end of thread, and put the tip of your awl in the centre of the loop, right next to the bead. Tighten the loop by taking up slack as you pull the thread until it knots firmly around the awl. Use your fingernail as leverage to hold the knot tight against the bead as you release the awl. Put a dab of G-S Hypo Cement or glue on the thread with the tip of a straight pin, let it dry for a few minutes, and trim with scissors or wire cutters.

Jump to It

To open and close a jump ring, first hold the jump ring with a pair of chain-nose or bent chain-nose pliers, so that the seam of the jump ring is at the top of the ring and the side of the jump ring is being held in the pliers. With another pair of pliers, grasp the other side of the ring. Holding one hand steady, rotate the other set of pliers away from you so that the jump ring opens. Rotate the pliers towards you to close the jump ring. Never pull the jump ring apart as this will stretch the circle and make it difficult to maintain the round shape.

easy
★

swinging style

Flexible beading wire is most often used for necklaces and bracelets, but here is a way to make simple, modern earrings. Using silver-plated wire instead of standard beading wire brightens the colour of the hoop from dull grey to shiny silver, perfectly complementing the zingy bead combinations.

Materials

Beads:
  2 crimp beads
  52 x Size 12 delica beads
  2 x 9mm fluted barrel
  beads
2 x 15cm (6in) lengths of
  flexible beading wire, size
  medium
Crimping pliers
Pair of ear wires
Wire cutters
Chain-nose or bent chain-
  nose pliers

1 Slide a crimp bead onto the spool of beading wire, followed by 13 delica beads, one barrel bead and then 13 more delica beads. Take the tail of the wire and thread it back through the crimp bead, making a teardrop shape approximately 2cm (¾in) wide, and 3cm (1¼in) long under the crimp bead. Take up any slack from the spool end instead of the tail end to conserve wire. Leave the wire tail about 2cm (¾in) long.

2 Hold the earring between your fingertips right under the crimp bead. Turn the tail of the wire under and back through the crimp bead, forming a loop. Pull so that the loop measures about 4cm (1½in) long.

3 Put the crimp bead in the crimping pliers parallel to the loop. Crimp the bead, then trim the excess wire.

4 Repeat Steps 1–3 for the second earring. To finish, attach the loops to ear wires, using chain-nose or bent chain-nose pliers to open and close the jump rings.

Kink-free

Thread the needle with the thread still on the spool, instead of cutting the thread first. This helps the grain of the thread go in the right direction, and makes the thread less likely to kink.

easy
★

mint chip
necklace

A strand of simple beads is a perfect way to introduce you to bead stringing with needle and thread. You can draw inspiration for your colour schemes from anywhere – mint choc chip ice cream (my favourite flavour) inspired this colour palette.

Materials

2 flexible wire needles,
 Size 10 or 8
Beading thread, such as
 C-Lon Micro, 0.12mm
Beads:
 4 x 4mm round metal
 spacer beads (Bead A)
 32 x 10mm round beads
 (Bead B)
 50 x 10mm spacer beads
 (Bead C)
2 x 1cm (½in) lengths of
 French wire
2 x 4mm jump rings
Wire cutters
Beading awl
22mm j-hook clasp
G-S Hypo Cement or strong
 glue

1 Thread the needle with 1.5m (60in) thread. Make a slip knot. Stretch the thread overnight by hanging an object weighing about 0.5kg (1lb) from the loop.

2 Slide on a Bead A, then a length of French wire and a jump ring. Gently pull the needle and thread back through the hole of Bead A nearest the French wire, so that the wire loop encloses the jump ring. Add another Bead A.

3 String beads in the following sequence: BB, CC, B, CCC, until you have strung all the beads. Then string two Bead A, followed by a length of French wire and a jump ring. Cut the needle and grasp the jump ring following the instructions on pages 23–24.

4 Slide the beads down towards the loop you've just made, undo the slip knot at the other end and pick up the slack by pulling the thread until the French wire loop meets the last bead. Make a knot with your awl and fingernail.

5 Pull the thread through Bead A and the nearest Bead B. If the thread is too short to easily go back through the bead, trim the needle. Trim the thread close to the bead, and glue the knot.

6 To finish the necklace, attach the clasp to one of the jump rings and secure.

In Sequence

To help you remember the sequence of the beads, you can use a bead board or tray to lay out the pattern in the channels before you begin. They also have small compartments to store the beads as you work.

mint chip necklace   33

advanced
★★★

moss rose bracelet

The delicate colours of salmon and pale yellow of the moss rose are illustrated in this triple strand bracelet. Instead of mixing the beads on each strand, I chose single strands of beads in different colours, shapes and finishes so that each type of bead gets equal billing.

Materials

Makes a 19cm (7½in) bracelet

Size 8 flexible wire needles
Nylon beading thread, such
    as C-Lon Micro, 0.12mm
Beads:
    12 x 3mm silver spacer
    beads (Bead A)
    24 x 6mm iridescent finish
    beads (Bead B)
    9 x 14mm x 8mm pebble
    shaped beads (Bead C)
    14 x 10mm round beads
    (Bead D)
    2 x 11 x 12mm bead cones
6 x 1cm (½in) lengths of
    French wire
15mm toggle closure
3 x 4mm jump rings
Wire cutters
G-S Hypo Cement or strong
    glue
12cm (4¾in) length of
    24 gauge silver wire
Scissors

1 Thread a needle with 70cm (27½in) of thread, doubling up the thread and closing with a slip knot at the end. Make a slip knot. Stretch the thread overnight by hanging an object weighing about 0.5kg (1lb) from the loop.

2 String on one Bead A, then a length of French wire. Hold the French wire gently as you slide it on, as it may catch the fibres of the thread and snag. Pass the needle back through the hole of Bead A that is closest to the French wire. This will form a French wire loop (see page 23).

3 String on one more Bead A, then 22 Bead B, then two Bead A to make a bracelet measuring 19cm (7½in). To adjust for a smaller or larger bracelet, add or subtract more silver beads. Then slide on a piece of French wire followed by a jump ring.

4 Cut the eye of the needle with wire cutters and remove the needle from the thread. Hold your thumb, forefinger and index finger together, and drape the loop of the thread over them. Pull the French wire with your free hand up towards your fingers following the instructions on page 24, until the French wire contains the jump ring.

5 Slide the beads, except for the last two silver beads, down towards the loop you made with the French wire and follow the instructions on page 24 to tie a knot in the end of the thread. Put the tails through the eye of another needle and pass the needle through the two beads that are closest to the knot. Trim the thread, and put a dab of G-S Hypo Cement or glue on the knot.

6 Repeat Steps 1–5 for Bead C and Bead D strands.

7 Remove all the jump rings from the French wire loops. Take a 6cm (2½in) piece of silver wire and make a loop. Slide the French wire loops of each strand onto the loop, and close. Slide on a bead cone, then a Bead B. Close with a wire-wrapped loop. Repeat for the other end of the bracelet.

8 Attach one jump ring to each wire-wrapped loop, and attach your toggle closure to the jump rings.

moss rose bracelet   37

wraparound beaded lariat

Czech glass beads have been made for centuries, and come in a fantastic array of shapes, sizes and colours. Here, I use some favourite vintage styles: translucent faceted cathedral beads, opaque barrels in a pure sea blue and two-toned fluted beads for a twenties-style lariat worthy of the best tea dress.

Materials

Makes a 96cm (38in) lariat
Wire cutters
1.5m (60in) flexible beading
  wire, size medium or fine
Beads:
  59 x 5 x 4mm barrel beads
  (Bead A)
  113 x 6 x 8mm crystal
  cathedral-shaped beads
  (Bead B)
  17 x 9mm fluted beads
  (Bead C)
  20 x 3 x 2mm spacer
  beads (Bead D)
  6 x barrel-shaped crimp
  beads
Crimping pliers
2 head pins

1 Cut a piece of beading wire about 114cm (45in) long. String on a crimp bead about 5cm (2in) from the end, and hold it steady with your thumb and forefinger. Pass the end of the beading wire through the crimp bead and adjust the slack so that you have a small loop measuring approximately 3mm in interior diameter. Crimp the crimp bead with your pliers, and trim the excess wire.

2 String your beads on the beading material in the following sequence: A, BB, C, BB, A, BB, AA, BB. Follow this sequence 14 times, then string on a crimp bead, and then about 18 to 20 spacer beads (Bead D), or enough so that your largest bead will hang centrally.

3 Next, pass the end of the beading wire back through the crimp bead and nearest Bead B. Hold the newly formed beaded loop and pull the beading wire firmly with your other hand to tighten the slack. Crimp the bead next to the loop, and then cut away the excess wire.

4 Cut a 15cm (6in) length of beading wire, form a small loop at the end and crimp a crimp bead. Slide on beads in the following sequence: B, C, B, AA, BB, then slide on a crimp bead. Pass the end of the beading wire through the loop on the end of the long, beaded strand from Step 2, and then back though the crimp bead and Bead B. Crimp, and trim the excess wire, attaching this short strand to the small wire loop of the long strand of beads.

5 Repeat with another 15cm (6in) length of wire, this time with a bead sequence of: A, B, C, BB, A, BB, AA.

6 To finish the necklace, attach one Bead C to the end loops of the two short beaded strands. Do this by wire wrapping a bead onto a head pin and then attach to each loop of beading wire.

Cap It

If you have beads with large holes, consider using bead caps with the bead. These will prevent tiny accent or spacer beads being swallowed by the hole.

wraparound beaded lariat 41

advanced
★★★

gilded flowers

Czech glass flowers give a vintage flair to this triple strand necklace with an elegant but simple pattern of repeats. Flexible beading wire makes this quick and easy to make, leaving you time to try out different colour schemes for different outfits.

Materials

Wire cutters
Flexible beading wire, size
  medium
Crimping pliers
Beads:
  6 crimp beads
  Approx. 90 x 4mm faceted
  glass beads (Bead A)
  Approx. 82 x 6mm faceted
  glass beads (Bead B)
  Approx. 46 x 8mm flower
  beads (Bead C)
6 open jump rings
Barrel clasp

1 Cut three sections of beading wire, each measuring 50cm (19¾in). Take one section and crimp a bead to form a loop as described on page 20.

2 String your beads onto the first strand in this sequence: A, B, C, B, A. Continue this pattern 14 times, until you have a strand measuring about 40cm (15¾in). If you need a longer length, continue your bead sequence until it is long enough, but always ending with a Bead A. Make a loop at the end and crimp.

3 String the second strand following Steps 1–2, this time adding one sequence more than the previous strand.

4 Continue with the third strand, again adding an extra sequence.

5 Add jump rings to each of the crimped end loops, leaving them slightly open so that you can easily attach the jump rings to the clasp.

6 Attach the shortest strand to one of the end loops on one of the two clasp pieces. Then add the second strand to the middle loop of the clasp. Follow with the third strand on the last loop of the clasp.

7 Attach the strands to the second part of the clasp in the same sequence, starting with the shortest strand and ending with the longest. Make sure that the clasp is oriented so that when it is closed, the ends of each strand meet the same ends of the same strand.

Tightly Grasped

When you are forming a loop with your crimp bead and wish to make it as tight as possible, grasp the beading wire with your round-nose pliers right above the crimp bead. Pull up the slack by pulling the tail of the beading wire.

wire wrapping

I started wire wrapping some time after stringing as a way to show off some pretty gemstone beads. Learning to wire wrap was an easy transition from bead stringing, since I had fine-tuned my hand skills that are needed to work the pliers in a small format. Jewellery made with wire-wrapped beads has become increasingly popular, and is accomplished by using beads and wrapped wire loops to construct necklaces, bracelets, rings and earrings. Wire-wrapped jewellery can be as simple as one beautiful bead wire-wrapped for an earring, or it can involve several time-consuming layers of beaded chain.

Making a rosary loop

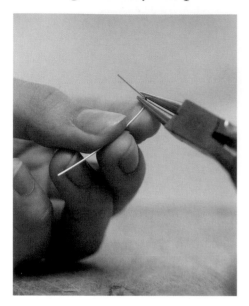
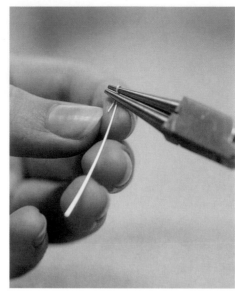

1 Bending

Cut a piece of wire about 5cm (2in) long. Hold the wire in the jaws of your round-nose pliers, about midway to one-third of the way up from the tip, depending on the fineness of the tip. Grasp the wire so that about 2cm (¾in) is sticking up. Make a right angle in the wire by bending the small section of wire towards you.

2 Forming the loop

With the finger and thumb of your other hand, bend the short tail of wire back over the top jaw of your pliers. Once the short end of the wire meets the long end underneath the pliers, remove the loop from the top jaw and place it on the bottom jaw, again one-third of the way from the tip.

3 Finishing the loop

Continue to bend the wire as you did before, crossing the short tail over the long tail of wire, making a 30-degree angle with the short tail and turning it away from you.

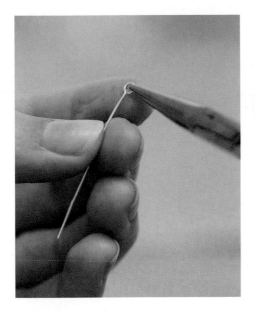

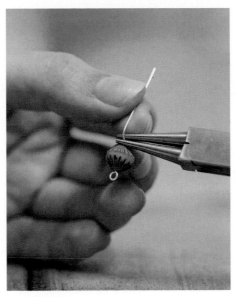

4 Adjusting

Using wire cutters, trim the short tail of wire at the base of the rounded loop. Use chain-nose or bent chain-nose pliers to adjust the loop open or closed. See page 25 for instructions on opening a loop.

5 Adding a bead

Slide on a bead, hold the loop flat between your thumb and forefinger, and bend the tail of wire towards you, as before. With the finger and thumb of your other hand, bend the short tail of wire back over the top jaw of your pliers.

Open or Closed?

Consider whether you would like to have an open loop to hook onto a separate piece.

6 Second loop

Once the short end of the wire meets the long end underneath the pliers, remove the loop from the top jaw and place it on the bottom jaw, again one-third of the way from the tip. Continue to bend the wire as you did before, crossing the short tail over the long tail of wire, making a 30-degree angle with the short tail and turning it away from you. Using wire cutters, trim the short tail of wire at the base of the rounded loop. Use chain-nose or bent chain-nose pliers to adjust the loop open or closed.

Making a closed wire-wrapped loop

Making a closed wire-wrapped loop is much the same as making a rosary loop, only with a few modifications in the final stages where you wrap the wire to secure the loop.

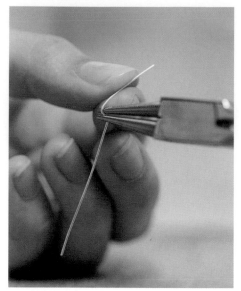

1 **Bending the wire**
For a wire-wrapped loop, start with a longer tail of wire, such as 2.5cm (1in). Make a right angle in the wire by bending the small section of wire towards you.

2 **Forming a loop**
With the finger and thumb from your other hand, bend the short tail of wire back over the top jaw of your pliers to form a loop. Once the short end of the wire meets the long end underneath the pliers, remove the loop from the top jaw and place it on the bottom jaw, again one-third of the way from the tip.

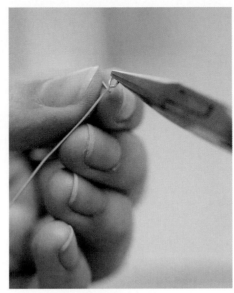

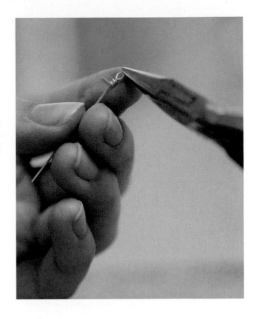

3 Crossing over the tail

Continue to bend the wire as you did before, crossing the short tail over the long tail of wire, making a 30-degree angle with the short tail and turning it away from you.

4 Wrapping

Instead of cutting the wire at the base of the loop, wrap the small tail of wire around the long tail at the base of the loop. Do this by grasping the top of the loop with your chain-nose pliers.

5 Twisting

With your other hand, twist the short tail of wire around the long end at the base of the loop. Twist the wire around the long end two or three times.

 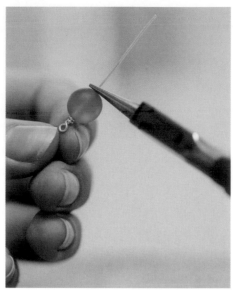 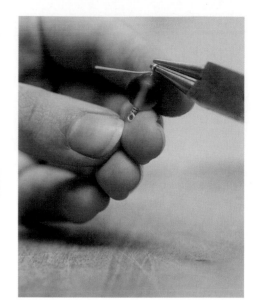

6 Trimming

Using wire cutters, cut the excess wire of the short end right next to the long piece of wire, under the wrapped coil.

7 Adding beads

Slide on the bead or beads you are using, and repeat Steps 2–5, making the initial right angle about 2mm from the top of the bead. Sometimes you might have a bead that has a larger hole than you would like, making for a bead that isn't held steady by the wire wrap. To correct the sliding, make a double wrap. When you put the wire in the jaws initially, leave a tail that is twice as long as before, about 4cm (1½in).

8 Second loop

Continue to bend the wire as you did before, crossing the short tail over the long tail of wire, making a 30-degree angle with the short tail and turning it away from you.

Breathing Space

While it is important that you wrap the wire close enough to hold the bead in place, be aware of wrapping too tightly. Some delicate beads may crack if they are put under too much pressure. Give your bead a little breathing space without it moving freely on the wire.

9 Wrapping the coil

Wrap your wire two or three times, as shown in Steps 4–5. Then, change direction of your wire wrapping, and wrap over the already-wrapped coil, heading back towards the loop.

10 Finishing

Using wire cutters, trim the short tail of wire at the top of the rounded loop. Use the tip of the round-nose pliers to push the end of the wire against the coil, below the loop.

Making a briolette loop

Briolettes are pretty teardrop-shaped beads that have side-drilled holes, instead of holes drilled from top to bottom. Briolettes are commonly made from gemstones, although those made from glass are also available. Several briolette wrapping methods are known, and I will demonstrate the one that works the best for me.

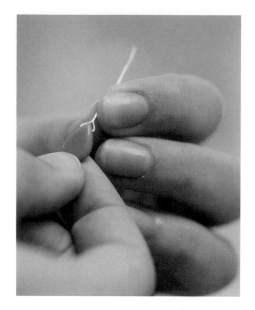

1 Threading

First cut a piece of 24 or 26 gauge wire, measuring about 8cm (3in) long. Slide on a briolette about two-thirds of the way down the wire. Pinch the wire together above the apex of the bead.

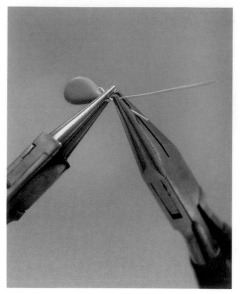

2 Twisting

Hold the apex of the wire with the round-nose pliers and use the bent-nose pliers to twist the wire together two or three times. Using wire cutters, cut the short end of the wire right above the twist.

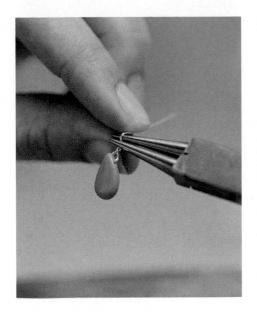

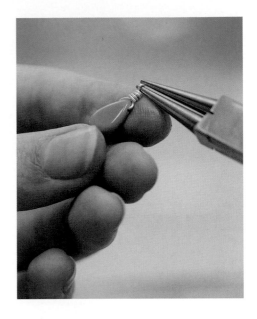

3 Forming a loop

Directly above the twist, bend the long piece of wire towards you. Make a wire wrapped loop. With the finger and thumb of your other hand, bend the short tail of wire back over the top jaw of your pliers to form a loop.

4 Wrapping wire

Once the short end of the wire meets the long end underneath the pliers, remove the loop from the top jaw and place it on the bottom jaw, again one-third of the way from the tip. Hold the loop with the chain-nose pliers, and wrap the tail of wire around the twisted section. Cut the excess wire.

5 Finishing

Use the round-nose pliers to push the end of the wire against the coil. The wrapped briolette can now be attached to your piece or to earring wires.

Practice Piece

Wrapping a briolette is a tricky technique that takes a bit of practice, so use copper wire or craft wire before you use sterling silver wire.

easy

★

beaded bloom ring

If you love rings and plan to make several, a steel ring mandrel is a wise investment and this project will be a great introduction to using one. Alternatively, you can buy a wooden dowel or find something around the house that is a size larger than your ring size. I used silver-coated copper wire for this ring, but it can also be made with half-hard sterling silver. Even though it's simple, it does take a little elbow grease, but it's so easy to make that the reward is well worth it.

Materials

Beads:
   Flat bead, about 15mm in
   diameter
   2 x 3mm faceted round
   glass beads
76cm (30in) length of
   20 gauge wire, plus extra
   for practice
Ring mandrel, dowel or a
   thick pen that is one size
   larger than your ring size
Chain-nose pliers
Needle file or sandpaper

1 Slide one small glass bead, the flat bead and another small glass bead to the halfway point of the length of wire. Pinch the wire between your two fingers so that it folds at a 90-degree angle to the largest bead, and hold the small beads steadily under the large bead.

2 Brace the mandrel in your lap, against a table. Place the bead and wire facing you on your mandrel at the mark that is one size larger than your ring size. Hold the wire as follows: in your left hand hold the wire that is on the right side of the mandrel, and in your right hand hold the wire that is on the left side of the mandrel, creating tension. You can steady your bead by pressing it with your thumbs as you wrap.

3 Crisscross the wire on the bottom part of the ring, keeping the wire flat against the mandrel. Bring the ends of the wire up the sides of the mandrel. Crisscross under the flat bead, changing hands. Immediately after you change hands, use your index finger and thumb nails to push the wire you just wrapped under the bead, towards the bead's centre. The small beads should be above the wire, next to the flat bead, as you head past them and towards the bottom of the ring.

4 Wrap the wire around the mandrel again, crisscrossing and changing hands while keeping the wire flat against the mandrel. Take the wire under the large bead again, and then wind both sides of the wire three times anticlockwise under the small beads.

5 Slide the ring carefully off the mandrel. Trim the wire so that about 4cm (1½in) of wire extends past the beads. With chain-nose pliers, pull one end of the wire through the shank (centre) of the ring, and wrap around the wire of the shank three times. Do the same for the other side of the ring. Trim the wire on the outside of the shank, and mash the cut end with your pliers so it won't snag. File away any roughness on the ends with a metal file or sandpaper.

beaded bloom ring   59

intermediate
★★

crystal tip earrings

Metallic-coated faceted glass beads create a timeless glamour when combined with gold-filled wire and chain. Fine curb chain creates movement when worn, and the facets add sparkle for a dressed-up look. If curb chain isn't available, a light cable chain makes a nice stand-in.

Materials

Beads:
   2 x 12 x 8mm crystal
   teardrop beads
   4 x 4mm Czech cube
   beads
   2 x 6mm faceted Czech
   beads
2 head pins
Round-nose pliers
26.5cm (10½in) length of
   curb chain
Wire cutters
30.5cm (12in) length of 24
   gauge gold-filled or plated
   wire
2 jump rings
Pair of ear wires

1 Put one teardrop bead onto each head pin. Create an open loop with your round-nose pliers. Attach a 1cm (½in) piece of curb chain to the loop, and close the loop.

2 Create an open loop with a 5cm (2in) piece of wire, and hook onto the piece of chain above the teardrop. Slide two cube beads onto this piece of wire, and create an open loop. Hook the wire onto a 1cm (½in) section of chain, and close the loop.

3 Cut a 7cm (2¾in) piece of wire. Create an open loop on one end of the wire and slide the beaded chain section onto this loop. On the short end of the loop, slide a 3cm (1¼in) section of the chain to rest against the beaded section. Next to this section, place a 2.5cm (1in) piece of chain. On the long end of wire, on the other side of the beaded section, slide a 2.5cm (1in) piece of chain. Next to this,

place a 2cm (¾in) piece of chain. Close the loop, then slide on a faceted 6mm bead. Close this loop, and attach a jump ring. Attach the jump ring to an ear wire.

4 Repeat Steps 1–3 for the second earring.

Short Cuts

Cutting small sections of wire can be tedious – here is a way to make it a little easier. Hold a straight pin horizontally with one hand and hang the length of chain from it. Hold a tape measure vertically next to the chain, grasping it with the same fingers that are holding the pin. With your free hand, cut the chain to the desired length with your wire cutters.

easy

★

caribe necklace

Simple glass beads in ocean colours are wire wrapped
to a silver chain to add an extra layer to this necklace.
Faceted cuts and frosty finishes on the beads mix up
the textures to give an added dimension to this versatile
piece that can be worn in the day or evening.

Materials

For a 40cm (16in) necklace
61cm (24in) length of
   24 gauge silver wire
Round, chain-nose and bent
   chain-nose pliers
Beads:
   8 x 8mm faceted beads
   (Bead A)
   7 x 10mm round beads
   (Bead B)
Wire cutters
2 jump rings
40.5cm (16in) length of chain
   with large (about 6mm)
   links with clasp

1 On the end of the length of wire, create a closed wire-wrapped loop to hold your beads (see page 50). Slide beads onto the spool of wire in the following sequence: A, B, A, B, AA, BBB, AA, B, A, B, A.

2 Create a closed loop on the other end of the length of wire. Slide up the closest bead and hold it along with the wire between your thumb and forefingers. Trim the wire about 2cm (¾in) below the bead. Create a closed loop.

3 Create an open loop, and hook to the bead with the closed loop you just made. Close the loop and slide up Bead B. Create a closed loop on the end of this bead. Continue the sequence of linking the beads together. When you have linked all of the beads together, attach a jump ring to each end of the beaded section.

4 Lay the chain down on a flat surface. Attach the jump rings of the beaded section about 11cm (4¼in) from each end of the chain (not including the clasp).

Shine Away

Sometimes brand new silver chain is a little too bright. To achieve a matt finish, go over the chain several times with a piece of fine steel wool or very fine sandpaper.

caribe necklace 67

easy

★

pearl cascade

These earrings feature a sumptuous cascade of glass pearls. They are also much easier to make than you would think. Sometimes you can find glass pearl mixes containing the perfect combination for the project. You can also use strands of inexpensive freshwater pearls with enough beads left over for a matching necklace.

Materials

Wire cutters
8cm (3in) length of chain
    with elongated links
    measuring about 5mm
    (¼in) each
Beads:
    14 x 8mm pearls (Bead A)
    14 x 6mm pearls (Bead B)
    14 x 4mm pearls (Bead C)
42 silver-toned head pins
Round-nose pliers
2 jump rings
Pair of ear wires

1 Cut the chain into two equal sections of 4cm (1½in) each. Place one pearl onto each of your 42 head pins. Make a rosary loop above each bead (see page 48), trim the excess wire, but don't worry yet about closing the loop completely.

2 On the end link on one of your chain sections, place beads in the following sequence: B, A, C, A. Close the wire loops with your pliers. On the following link, attach one Bead B on each side of the link. Repeat for the following link.

3 On the next link, attach one Bead C to each side of the link. Repeat this step for each subsequent link, until you reach the end of the chain. When you arrive at this end link, only attach one Bead C.

4 On the first link with the four pearls, attach a jump ring so that two pearls are on each side. Add the jump ring to an ear wire. Repeat Steps 2–4 for the second earring.

antique key necklace

This asymmetric necklace uses an antique skeleton key and vintage Czech glass flower beads, which are easier to find than you might think. If you do have trouble finding them, new Czech glass will work well. Flea markets and online sites such as ebay and etsy are great places to look for the materials in this project.

Materials

Wire cutters
Approx. 40.5cm (16in) length
of antiqued sterling silver
chain with links about 4mm
in diameter
Antiqued 22 gauge sterling
silver wire
Round-nose pliers
Beads:
2 x seed beads (Bead A)
8 x 4mm round red beads
(Bead B)
1 x 10mm pressed flower
cube bead (Bead C)
5 x flower bead caps
(Bead D)
Antiqued sterling silver jump
rings, 2 x 8mm and
2 x 4mm
Old skeleton key
Antiqued sterling silver clasp
and jump ring

1 Cut some links from your chain so that you have five closed links to serve as extra jump rings.

2 Wire wrap two Bead B to a closed link cut in Step 1, leaving a loop open, and then attach one link to each of the open loops. You'll have a tiny chain of two wrapped beads and three links at this point. Attach a wire-wrapped bead to each of your end links, followed by two links on either end. Your finished piece of chain will have five links and four beads. Attach one 4mm jump ring to each link.

3 Attach an 8mm jump ring to the top loop of the key, and one to the adjacent loop for the pendant to hang asymmetrically.

4 Cut a section of chain with four links (about 1cm/½in long), and a section of chain with sixteen links (about 4.5cm/1¾in long). Wire wrap one seed bead and Bead B to each of the jump rings on the key and attach a section of cut chain to the loops on each bead.

5 Attach Bead C to the smaller section of chain you cut in the last step, leaving the loop at the other end open. This side will now be known as the left side when you are working on it in front of you. To the larger link of chain, attach one Bead B, again leaving the loop at the other end open.

6 Cut five sections of chain of eight links, or 2.5cm (1in) each. Attach a section of chain to the open loop on Bead C, and attach a section of chain to Bead B on the other side of the necklace. On the side of the necklace with Bead C (the left side), attach a wire-wrapped Bead B, followed by a section of cut chain.

7 On the other side of the necklace (the right side), wire wrap two Bead D onto the chain, leaving one loop open. Attach another cut section of chain to the open loop, and wrap the loop closed. Switch to the left side of the necklace and repeat the wrapping of two Bead D.

Ageing Gracefully

To achieve an aged finish on sterling silver, peel two freshly hard-boiled eggs and put in a small sealable plastic bag. Mash the eggs well in the bag and then add the sterling silver wire, chain or findings. Close the bag and leave to tarnish. This can take anything from half an hour to several hours. Rinse the silver well. You can go over the silver with fine steel wool for a more varied antique finish.

8 Wire wrap a Bead B to the right side of the chain, leaving one loop open, and do the same on the left side. Attach a 10cm (4in) section of chain to one side, and a 9cm (3½in) section of chain to the other. Attach the clasp to the shorter piece of chain, and a jump ring to the longer side.

9 Wire wrap a Bead D right of centre on the decorative part of the key.

10 For the final step, attach the small chain of red beads from Step 2. Open the jump ring on one end, and attach it to a link just beneath Bead C. Attach the other side about four links below the first Bead B on the right side of the necklace.

polymer clay

My first experience with polymer clay was using it as a modelling material as a teenager. I made a hideous sea creature. Years later, I looked around and noticed that jewellery artists were making some pretty impressive pieces, pieces that I would love to wear and learn to make. You can utilise so many styles and methods working with polymer clay, making it a versatile complement to jewellery techniques such as wire wrapping and stringing. I've included some basic techniques in this chapter to get you started.

Conditioning the clay

Before you make any project, it will be necessary to condition the clay. This process of kneading, warming and rolling the clay, several times, helps to make the clay stronger after baking. All brands of polymer clay require conditioning before you start designing and baking. Always ensure that there aren't any air bubbles in the clay – these will burst and ruin your piece when baked.

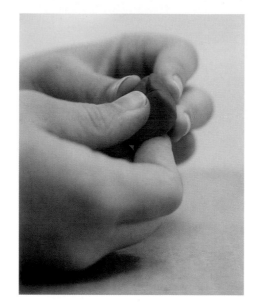

1 Kneading
Start by playing with the clay much as you might have done with regular clay in art class. First, pinch off a piece of clay from your pack that is the right size for your project. Knead the clay between your thumb and first two fingers. The clay will start to soften as you work with it.

2 Rolling
When the consistency of the clay has gone from crumbly to soft, roll the clay into an even, smooth ball between your fingers (this feels very therapeutic!).

3 Twisting the clay

When the ball is smooth, roll it out on a clean, flat surface into a snake-like length. Next, double the length and, holding each end, twist into a doubled rope.

4 Warming the clay

Roll the twisted coil into a ball again between your hands. Then roll the ball into a coil, repeating the twist, and then back into a ball. Your clay should be warm and glossy at this stage.

5 Rolling out

Let the clay rest for a minute, and then roll it out with the roller to the desired thickness for your project. Always roll on a clean surface, such as your cutting mat, or on parchment paper.

Sticky Stuff

If the clay starts to stick to the roller or your work surface, go over the roller with a little alcohol, and let the clay rest for a minute to cool down from the heat of your hands.

Punching holes

1 Piercing

A stylus, awl or toothpick can be used to pierce holes and add patterns to the surface of the clay prior to firing. With a steady hand, push the stylus needle into the clay to leave a round impression or pattern on the surface. To widen holes, rotate the stylus very slightly when the tip reaches the work surface.

Transferring images

1 Placing image

Trim the image transfer paper to the correct size for your piece and place face down in position on the clay. Burnish lightly with your ring finger to ensure contact between the paper and the clay.

3 Revealing image

Carefully remove the backing paper, lifting it up squarely, to reveal the transferred image on the clay.

2 Wetting

Wet a paintbrush with water and lightly brush over the back of the paper, saturating the paper. You'll start to see the image appear through the paper. Put something lightweight on top of the paper to maintain contact, such as a pack of cards. Leave for 5 minutes, then brush over the image with water again. Leave for a further 10 minutes.

Cutting out

1 Trimming
To cut out or trim a shape from clay, use a straight edge ruler and sharp craft knife on a cutting mat. Most mats have ruled divisions to help you judge straight lines and achieve right-angled corners.

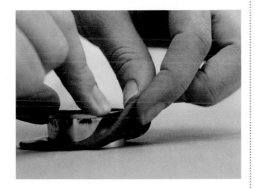

2 Using shape cutters
Once the clay is ready you can use it in a variety of ways. A cookie cutter is ideal for creating shapes that can be baked or embellished further.

Stamping in clay

1 Using a stamp
You can make impressions in clay, and create moulds, using special stamps or any object with a raised and patterned surface. Prepare the clay as before, rolling out to the desired thickness. Ensure that your stamp is clean before use.

2 Making an impression
Gently push the stamp into the clay surface, deep enough to cover the detailing around the borders if necessary. Lift the stamp away to reveal the impression. The clay can be embellished further, trimmed and baked as required.

Smooth Operator

To remove fingerprints or marks, gently smooth them with your ring finger. If, after baking, you find fingerprints, sand them smooth. To sand smooth edges, use a 600 or 800 grit sandpaper dipped in water (to avoid creating dust). Sand in one direction for best results and sand before glazing. Avoid sanding transferred image areas.

easy

★

cherry blossom hairpins

These pretty hairpins combine exotic yuzen origami paper with a simple polymer clay backing. Yuzen paper, also known as Chiyogami, has a heavier weight than basic origami paper, and is able to withstand several coats of polymer glaze without tearing or wrinkling. Yuzen paper comes in countless patterns from traditional florals to mosaics or geometric repeats, and uses gold and silver foil in many of the designs.

Materials

Yuzen washi paper (origami
  paper)
Oval clay cutters or template
Pencil
Scissors
Glossy polymer glaze
Parchment paper and cutting
  mat
Alcohol and pad
Acrylic rolling pin
5g polymer clay
Tweezers
Awl or toothpick
Oven and oven thermometer.
Baking sheet
400 grit sandpaper
e6000 glue or two-part epoxy
Craft knife
2 hairpins

1 Hold the origami paper up to the light to establish which parts of the design you want to cut out. On the back of the paper, trace around an oval clay cutter or template with a pencil over your selected areas to give you two ovals.

2 Cut the ovals out carefully with small scissors. Coat the oval pieces of origami paper on both sides with the glossy glaze, allowing it to dry for 30 minutes between sides.

3 Tape a piece of parchment paper to a cutting mat. With an alcohol-soaked pad, lightly go over the parchment paper, the rolling pin and your fingers to remove small bits of dust that may imbed in the clay, and leave to dry. Condition the clay by rolling between your fingers for a few minutes (see page 78).

4 Roll out the clay to a thickness of about 3mm. Use the oval clay cutter to cut out two oval shapes. With the tweezers, carefully centre each origami paper oval onto a polymer oval. Tap down lightly with your finger in the middle of the paper, then go around the edge of the paper oval and press the paper with an awl or toothpick so that the edge is flush with the clay.

5 Preheat the oven to the temperature specified on the polymer clay instructions. Use an oven thermometer to correctly read the temperature.

6 Cut out the piece of parchment paper around the ovals, so that you don't have to touch them with your fingers. Transfer the paper and clay ovals to a baking sheet and bake according to the polymer clay pack instructions. After the specified time, remove the baking sheet from the oven and allow to cool.

7 Sand the edges of the baked clay ovals with sandpaper. Apply three to four coats of glossy glaze to the paper only, allowing it to dry between coats.

8 Score the back of the polymer oval, to allow the glue to adhere. Apply the glue to a hairpin pad and then press the polymer disc onto it. Allow the glue to dry overnight, or according to glue manufacturer's iinstructions.

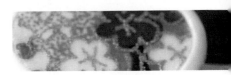

springtime in holland pendant

Inlaid tulips are created by first baking the tulip elements, and then inlaying the cured tulips into raw clay, and baking again. Use this technique anytime you want to achieve an inlaid or mosaic-type effect.

Materials

Oven and oven thermometer
Strong tape
Parchment paper and cutting
   mat
Polymer clay packs in red,
   white and light green
Acrylic rolling pin
Small oval clay cutter,
   9 x 13mm
Baking sheet
Craft knife
Tweezers
Awl
400 grit sandpaper
Glossy polymer glaze
Jump ring

1 Preheat the oven to the temperature specified on the polymer clay instructions. Use an oven thermometer to correctly read the temperature.

2 Tape a piece of parchment paper to a craft mat. Pull off one-quarter of a pack of the green clay (approximately 7g), and condition the clay until it is pliable. Roll it into a ball, and then roll it out into a sheet with a thickness of about 1.5mm. Cut out the parchment around the clay sheet, and set aside.

3 Tape down another piece of parchment, and roll 5g of the red clay into a 1.5mm thick sheet. Cut out ten or so ovals with the oval cutter, or with steady hands. Cut each oval in half. Remove the excess red clay, and cut out the parchment paper under the red half ovals.

4 Place the parchment paper holding the red half ovals and the paper holding the green clay, onto a baking sheet, and bake according to the polymer clay pack instructions. After the specified time, remove the baking sheet from the oven and allow to cool.

5 When completely cool, cut the green polymer clay into several strips 1.5mm wide and 3cm (1¼in) and 4cm (1½in) long, using a craft knife. Cut two wide v-shaped notches, meeting in the centre, into the flat top of each half circle, creating a tulip shape.

6 Condition and roll a 25g (1oz) piece of white clay to a thickness of 2.5–3mm.

7 Set the flowers into the clay as follows: select a 4cm (1½in) green stem and, with tweezers, set it vertically into the white clay, at least 3mm from any edge. Top the green stem with a red flower head. Tap each part very lightly into the soft clay to hold it in place. Pick out a red flower top and place it 1mm or so to the right of the flower. The top of this flower should line up with the centre of the first flower. Select a 3cm (1¼in) stem and place it under the flower head. Lightly tap with your tweezers to hold it in place.

8 Next, take a small piece of parchment paper and lay it over the clay. Rub your fingers over the paper several times, pushing the flowers gently into the soft clay. Cut out a rectangle around the flowers, leaving 8mm from the top of the tulips to the edge of the clay, 3mm from the bottom, and 2mm from each edge. Round the corners after you've cut the rectangle. Pierce a hole 3mm from the top edge with an awl.

9 Bake according to the polymer clay pack instructions. After baking, allow to cool and then sand the edges with wet sandpaper, or with a dremel and felt wheel if you have one.

10 Coat with glossy glaze, attach the jump ring and then attach the pendant to a necklace chain.

Clean Cut

To make the cutter glide easily when cutting clay, dip the cutter in a little water before making your cut.

advanced
★★★

cameo brooch

Here, the polymer clay takes on a matt, bisque texture in this Wedgwood-inspired brooch, perfect for adding a touch of elegance to a scarf or wrap. A flexible mould, which you can use many times, is easily made from a vintage plastic cameo for this project.

Materials

Old cameo or button
Mould-maker polymer clay, or
   regular clay for mould
Oven and oven thermometer
Polymer clay in two colours
Razor or clay blade
Parchment paper and cutting
   mat
Awl or toothpick
400 grit sandpaper
Acrylic rolling pin
Clay gun or extruder
   (optional)
Craft knife
e6000 glue
Brooch pin

1 Using a cameo or any other object, create a mould according to the manufacturer's directions. Preheat the oven to the temperature specified on the polymer clay instructions. Use an oven thermometer to correctly read the temperature.

2 Mist the mould lightly with water. Put a little clay ball or strip into the mould, and gently press the clay into the mould, working from the centre out. Gently press around the edges of the mould to make sure the outline of your polymer piece remains sharp. Trim any excess clay.

3 To release the mould, turn the mould over onto the piece of parchment paper. Flex the mould all around the edges to release the clay. After releasing, you can very gently smooth imperfections with your fingertips (your ring finger is best) and accentuate faint details with an awl or toothpick.

4 Bake according to the polymer clay pack instructions, and leave to cool. File any rough edges with wet fine grit sandpaper.

5 Condition about 4g of clay in a contrasting colour, then roll out an oval for the backing of the bust. Press the bust into the clay so that the edges go into the surface of the raw clay. Roll two skinny (approximately 2mm wide) 'snakes' with the polymer coil, long enough to wrap around the oval, plus at least 4.5cm (1¾in). Or, use a clay gun or extruder to do the work for you.

6 Wind the snakes together, starting from both ends, so that it resembles rope. Drape around the oval, and cut each end of the rope at an angle where it meets. Touch the ends together. Go around the rope with your awl, and gently touch the underside of each twist to the oval background. Cut out the square of paper on which the cameo lies, and bake according to pack instructions.

7 Remove from the oven and leave to cool. Using a strong glue, glue the brooch pin to the back of the cameo. Leave to dry.

Close Shave

When making a mould, it's better to put too little clay in to start with, and then add to it if needed. The clay should not spill over the edges. If it does, shave off the excess raw clay with a razor or clay blade.

intermediate
★★

lucky charm bracelet

With a horeshoe and four-leaved clover, your luck should be guaranteed with this simple charm on a rustic bracelet. This project uses a transfer technique with a toner-based print on paper. You can take your favourite image and photocopy it, to achieve the effect. Use only toner-based prints, since inkjet prints will not work for this project. The cheaper and more basic the copy machine, the better the results.

Materials

For polymer charm:
Oven and oven thermometer
Heart-shaped template (below)
Parchment paper, pencil and
    cutting mat
Craft knife or small scissors
Strong tape
5g polymer clay
Acrylic rolling pin
Black toner-based illustration
    on copy paper
Paintbrush and water
Tweezers
Awl or stylus
Baking sheet
400 grit sandpaper
Glossy polymer glaze
8mm jump ring

For 19cm (7½in) bracelet:
2 crimp beads
25.5cm (10in) length of
    flexible beading wire, size
    medium
Crimping pliers
4 x 5mm jump rings
Beads:
    12 x 4mm metal beads
    (Bead A)
    11 x 8mm metal beads
    (Bead B)
Wire cutters
Toggle clasp

1 Preheat the oven to the temperature specified on the polymer clay instructions. Use an oven thermometer to correctly read the temperature.

2 Trace the heart template below with a pencil on to a small piece of parchment paper. Cut out carefully with a craft knife or small scissors. Tape a large piece of parchment paper to a cutting mat with strong tape.

3 Condition and roll out a piece of clay about 1mm thick. Lay the image face down onto the raw clay, and burnish for a few seconds with your ring finger to establish good contact between the raw clay and paper. Follow the instructions on page 80 for transferring an image.

4 Carefully lift off the paper from the clay, revealing the transferred image. With your tweezers, centre the parchment paper heart over the image, and very gently place it on the clay. Go along the edge of the paper with the tweezers to secure. Trace around the heart with a sharp craft knife, cutting the clay. Carefully lift off the parchment heart with tweezers. Remove any excess clay and pierce a hole in the top portion of the heart with an awl.

5 Soften the edge of the clay with your ring finger and cut out the parchment paper underneath the heart in a square around the heart to avoid touching the raw clay. Place in the oven on a baking sheet, and bake according to the polymer clay pack instructions.

6 Allow to cool, then sand any rough edges with wet sandpaper. Apply two to four coats of glossy polymer glaze. Attach the heart to the 8mm jump ring.

7 Slide a crimp bead onto the length of flexible beading wire, hold it about 5cm (2in) from the end, and slide on a 5mm jump ring. Pass the short end of beading wire back though the crimp bead, leaving a tail just long enough to pass through a Bead A. Crimp the bead and slide on another Bead A, over both the long and short tail piece of beading wire. Trim the short piece of wire flush to the bead hole.

8 String on a Bead B and follow with a Bead A. Continue the sequence until you have a total of 12 Bead A and 11 Bead B, ending with a Bead A. Then, slide on a crimp bead and a jump ring, and pass the end of the beading wire back through the crimp bead and the nearest Bead A. Pull firmly to take up slack and crimp the bead. Trim the beading wire flush to Bead A as you did on the other end of the bracelet.

9 Link a jump ring to another jump ring, and attach to one end of the bracelet, so that you have three jump rings linked together. Attach the round part of the clasp to the end jump ring. Attach the heart charm to the centre jump ring. On the other end of the bracelet, attach the bar part of the toggle clasp to the end jump ring.

easy

★

tropical medley

The versatility of polymer clay lends itself well to this nature-inspired project. With coral reefs endangered across the globe, coral-coloured clay and glass beads come together for a beach-worthy necklace and matching earrings.

Materials

Makes a 51cm (20in) necklace

Oven and oven thermometer
25g red polymer clay
Acrylic rolling pin
Parchment paper
35mm round cutter
15mm round cutter
Stylus and embossing set
   with small, medium and
   large stylus, or pointed
   items such as straight pins,
   awls and toothpicks with a
   variety of diameters
Baking sheet
Beads:
   11 x 6mm blue glass beads
   1 x 6mm red glass bead
7mm jump ring
Silver-toned chain, link size
   about 4mm, cut into the
   following six sections:
   1 x 10cm (4in) section
   1 x 14cm (5½in) section
   3 x 2.5cm (1in) sections
   1 x 4cm (1½in) section
Silver-toned round wire
Wire cutters
Round-nose pliers
Bent-nose pliers
4 silver-toned head pins
Clasp with two jump rings

1 Preheat the oven to the temperature specified on the polymer clay instructions. Use an oven thermometer to correctly read the temperature.

2 Pinch off about one-third of the pack of polymer clay and condition the clay. Roll out the clay onto parchment paper to a thickness of about 3mm. Using the larger round cutter, pierce a circle into the clay. Do the same with the small cutter five times, so that you end up with five small circles and one large circle.

3 Pierce a hole in the top centre of the large circle for the jump ring. Follow by randomly piercing 10–15 holes with the largest stylus into the large circle of clay. Pierce just a few large holes into each of the small circles. Next, fill in each circle with smaller holes by continuing to punch circles randomly with the medium and small stylus. When you punch

the holes into the small circles, make sure you have two holes on the edge of the circles that directly face each other.

4 Transfer the circles and parchment paper to a baking sheet and bake according to the polymer clay pack instructions. Leave to cool.

5 Attach the 7mm jump ring to the top centre hole on the large circle. If the hole isn't completely punched through, use an awl to widen it.

6 Wire wrap a blue bead (see page 52), and attach it to the jump ring. Next, attach the jump ring to the 4cm (1½in) section of chain, about 2cm (¾in) from one end. The short end of the chain should be on the right side of the front, punched part of the circle.

7 On one small circle, thread a 7cm (2¾in) piece of wire through one of the two holes on the bottom edge. Using round-nose pliers, bend and grasp the wire together and make a twist 2–3mm close to the edge of the small circle. Trim one side of the wire. Slide a blue bead over the twist. Create a wire-wrapped loop. Repeat for the hole on the other edge. Repeat for all the small circles. Attach the loop to the short end of the chain attached to the large circle. Attach the other end to one of the 2.5cm (1in) sections of chain.

8 Attach a wire-wrapped blue bead to the end of the chain you attached to the first small disc, and then attach a 2.5cm (1in) section of chain to the other loop of this bead. Attach another small circle and bead section to this piece of chain, as you did in Step 7. Attach the 10cm (4in) section of chain to the bead.

9 Working now to the left of the pendant, attach a blue bead to the free link of chain. On the other loop of the blue bead, attach the last section of 2.5cm (1in) chain. Attach the last small circle section to this piece of chain, and than attach the 14cm (5½in) piece of chain to that.

10 Attach two blue beads and one red bead with a wire-wrapped head pin each to a link in this long piece of chain. Place them so that the cluster hangs directly across the last circle on the other side of the necklace. Attach the clasp to the end of the chain.

textiles

Textiles are generally not the first thing to come to mind when thinking of making jewellery. However, with a little knowledge of needle felting, sewing and some experience with crocheting, you'll be able to make fun and modern jewellery pieces you won't find in a typical jewellery store.

Hand sewing

Needle felting

1 Straight stitch

To sew a straight or running stitch by hand, thread a needle with a comfortable amount of thread, approximately 1m (39in) long. Double the thread and tie an overhand knot at the end of the thread. Bring the needle up through the two pieces of fabric from the back, and take it back down again approximately 5mm (¼in) to the right. Continue in a straight line with evenly spaced stitches. When you are out of thread, tie off by making an overhand knot on the back of the fabric.

1 Pulling

Pinch a small amount of wool from the wool top and fluff it up by pulling a few strands of wool fleece apart with your finger and thumb. Repeat a few times so that the wool piece loosely measures about 4.5cm (1¾in) square.

2 Rolling a ball

Once the piece of wool is the correct size and the fibres sufficiently separated, roll the wool into a very loose ball between your fingers, trying not to exert any pressure or compress the wool.

 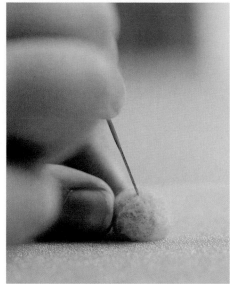 

3 Felting

Pinch the wool together into a small ball and place it on a foam felting mat. Hold it by one side and very carefully begin to felt the wool by poking the fluff with the felting needle. Push the felting needle far enough through the wool so that the barbs on the needle are coming into contact with the foam mat. Watch your fingers! Roll the wool around on the mat as you felt, so that the felt takes on a ball shape and you work on all sides.

4 Firming

As the part you are felting begins to firm, roll the ball a little to reveal a fuzzier section and felt again until firm. As you finish, you don't need to poke the needle all the way through. Firm up any surface fuzzy spots by poking with the needle.

5 Smoothing

While it isn't always necessary, you can smooth excess fuzziness. Put a drop of detergent in a cup or glass and add hot water. Wet the felted ball in the soapy water, and roll between your fingers to smooth the fibres and maintain the ball shape. Rinse briefly in hot water and allow to dry.

Crocheted beads

You will need:
Perle cotton #5 in assorted colours
Size 1 (2.00mm) steel crochet hook
Wooden beads about 1cm (½in) in
   diameter

Key:
ch = chain stitch
sc = single crochet
st = stitch

Note: To prevent tangles in the thread, wind
   the hanks into balls before beginning.

Decreasing

You may find that you need to
decrease more sharply. To do this, just
eliminate decrease round 2.

1 Making a circle
To begin, make a slip knot, ch 4 and join into a circle by making a slip st in the fourth st from the hook.

2 Continuing round
Round 1: ch 1, then 8 sc into the ring. **Round 2:** 2 sc into each st. **Round 3:** *1 sc, 2 sc. Repeat from * around.

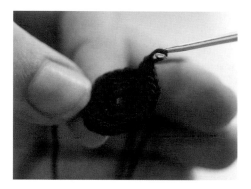

3 Increasing each round
For the next three to five rounds (depending on the size of the bead), make 1 sc in each st. At this point, fit the wooden bead into the crochet work. Your work should fit snugly around the bead, with about half of the bead covered. The remaining rows will be worked with the crochet work wrapped around the bead. If the crochet work does not yet reach the halfway point, work even rounds until it covers half of the bead.

4 Covering the bead
Begin to decrease rounds. **Decrease round 1:** *4 sc, skip the fifth st and 1 sc in the next st. Repeat from * around. **Decrease round 2:** sc around. **Decrease round 3:** *2 sc, skip the third st and sc in the next st. **Decrease round 4:** *sc, skip the next st. Repeat from * until the bead is completely covered, leaving a small hole at the top that aligns with the hole in the bead. Break the thread and weave in the loose ends.

Embellishing a felted bead

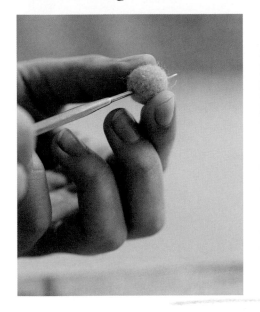

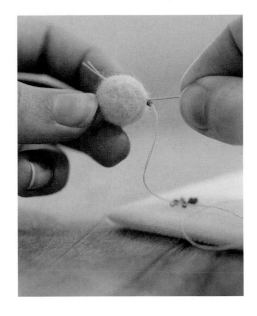

1 Piercing a hole

You can use your felted bead in many ways, either as a simple, plain bead or by embellishing with delicate seed beads to create a pretty, textured surface. Using an awl, pierce a hole through the centre of the felted bead. The bead is now ready to be used or embellished.

2 Threading

To add beads to the felted ball, tie a knot in a matching coloured thread and pull the needle and thread through the felt firmly so that the knot goes into the surface of the felt. Trim the ends of the thread.

3 Beading

Slide a bead onto the thread, bring the needle out through the surface of the ball and then back through the ball next to the bead to secure the bead on the surface. Continue to add further beads and when finished tie a knot above the last bead before you pull the thread through the felted ball. Trim the ends.

sprinkle sparkle ring

This cute little ring takes the simple felted ball a step beyond. Colourful beads and sequins adorn the dome, much as frosting and sprinkles festoon your favourite cupcake. This is a very simple and satisfying project and you'll probably get requests from many admirers for variations – it can easily be adapted to earrings, a pendant or just as a decoration on a bag or brooch.

Materials

Small amount of wool tops,
   merino or corriedale
   preferred
Felting needle, Size 36 or 38
Foam felting mat
Xacto knife or razor blade
Scissors
Perle cotton thread #5
Small sewing needle
Approximately 50 glass delica
   beads, size 11/0 in two
   colours
4 small sequins
Strong craft glue
Silver-toned adjustable ring
   blank

1 Felt a 2cm (¾in) ball (see page 105). Slice the felted ball in half with an xacto knife or razor blade, so that you have two domes. Put one aside for another project.

2 Cut a 102cm (40in) length of thread, thread the needle and double the thread. Tie a double knot at the end of the thread.

Bonus Ball

With the remaining half dome, a pendant for a necklace can be made by sewing a jump ring to the top back of the dome. Embellish the dome in the same way as the ring.

3 Hold the felted dome flat side up with one hand and with your other hand, pierce the dome with your needle about 2mm from the edge. From the back, flat side, pull the thread through until the knot catches. Slide a glass bead onto the needle and bring it down to the surface of the dome. Put the tip of the needle next to where the bead is sitting, at a bead's width distance from the bead. Make sure that the bead holes are horizontal to the edge of the dome instead of vertical. Pull the needle through. Push the needle a bead's width through the back, so that the needle will come through the front about 1mm above the first bead.

4 Put another glass bead, the same colour as the first, on the needle and move it down the thread so it is right next to the first bead. Pierce the felt with the needle, right next to the first bead, and while holding the bead so the holes are again horizontal to the edge, pull the needle through to the back.

5 Continue with a third bead, this time of the second colour. Pull the bead all the way down to the felt, and pierce the needle again, pulling the thread through and making sure that the bead is horizontally right next to the previous bead. Holding the dome curved side up, continue sewing the beads all along in a random pattern while making sure that the colours are balanced. After you have come back to the beginning, knot the thread next to the surface of the flat part of the dome and trim the excess thread.

6 After you have sewn on your border, begin sewing the centre part of the ring. Thread a needle with a 76cm (30in) length of thread, double it and tie a knot. Pierce through the centre of the dome from the back with your needle. Slide on a sequin, and then a bead. Push your needle back through the sequin hole, with the bead acting as a stopper. Sew about ten beads and four sequins close together in the centre randomly. Knot the back when you are finished, and trim the excess thread.

7 Glue the back of the finished piece to the ring blank. Enjoy!

sprinkle sparkle ring 111

easy

★

prairie print necklace

A strip of lightweight calico cotton is folded over, sewn, and stuffed with beads for a country-inspired necklace. A Liberty print cotton would also be great to use, or any other lightweight fabric. If you are an accomplished seamstress, this is a lovely project to use up any leftover fabric after making a dress, shirt or skirt for a coordinated look.

Materials

**Makes a 96cm (38in)
 necklace**
Lightweight cotton,
 9 x 110cm (3½ x 43in)
Beads:
 8 x 20mm wood beads
 (Bead A)
 7x 24mm wood beads,
 with at least a 9mm hole
 (Bead B)
Sewing machine
Needle and thread
Iron

1 Before you begin, make
sure that the fabric strip
will accommodate the 24mm
beads once it is sewn together.
Fold the fabric strip over the
bead and pinch together,
making sure you have a
minimum of 5cm (2in) to spare
on each side of the fabric.

2 Fold the strip of fabric in
half lengthways, right sides
together. Using a sewing
machine, sew the ends of the
fabric together with a straight
stitch and a 5mm (¼in) seam,
and continue sewing down the
length of the fabric until you
reach the midway point of the
strip. Leave a 4.5cm (1¾in)
opening large enough to
accommodate the beads, and
then continue sewing along the
edge of the fabric, and finish by
sewing the ends together.

3 Turn the fabric strip right
sides out. Roll one end of
fabric tightly so that the bead
will be able to pass through.
String on one Bead A over the
fabric, and slide it to within
5cm (2in) of the other end of
fabric. Next, insert a Bead A
into the opening, and slide this
bead down next to the first
bead. Continue with two more
Bead A in this manner, sliding
one over the fabric, followed by
inserting a bead into the
pocket. You'll finish with a Bead
A inside the fabric.

4 Follow the same method
for all seven of your Bead
Bs, starting and ending with a
Bead B slipped over the fabric.
Next, slide a Bead A inside the
fabric, and alternate as before,
using the remaining four
Bead A.

5 Hand sew the pocket
closed with a hand-sewn
blind stitch. Centre the beads
on the fabric strip, and tie a
knot above the last bead on
each end. Press the remaining
fabric flat, and tie a knot or bow
to secure around the neck.

easy

★

berry burst trio

Felted balls are so much fun! Colourful and quick to
make, needle-felted balls will add a unique texture to
your jewellery creations. I've added glass briolettes and
leaves for a fruity-themed project with a little glamorous
sparkle that will brighten any outfit.

Materials

**Makes a 45.5cm (18in)
   necklace**

Wool tops
Foam felting mat
Felting needle, Size 36 or 38
Household detergent and hot
   water
Beads:
   3 x glass briolettes or
   faceted teardrops
   3 x pressed glass leaves
   6 x seed or delica beads to
   match briolette
Round wire, 24 or 22 gauge
Chain-nose pliers
Round-nose pliers
Wire cutters
3 x 4mm jump rings
Necklace chain with clasp
Pair of ear wires

1 Make 3 felted beads by
following the instructions
on page 104.

2 String a seed bead onto
a length of wire, followed
by a felted wool bead, followed
by another seed bead. Repeat
twice.

3 On the end of the wire,
make a rosary loop and
cut off the excess (see page
48). Slide down a seed bead, a
felted bead and another seed
bead. Follow with a rosary loop
and trim the excess. Repeat
twice for the other beads on
the wire.

4 Using the briolette wrap
instructions on page 54,
attach a briolette bead to a loop
on a felted ball section.

5 Wire wrap a glass leaf (see
page 52) and attach it
along with the felted ball onto a
jump ring. Attach the jump ring
to your chain with the leaf
dangling in front of the ball.

6 Follow Steps 2–5 with the
two other balls, and then
attach the completed designs to
ear wires.

Marbled Mix

It's easy to create unique looks with felted beads. Instead of a
solid wool bead, try needle felting tiny amounts of different
coloured wools for a marbled effect. Small strands of wool yarn
can be appliquéd to the surface using a Size 38 or 40 felting
needle for a striped effect.

advanced
★★★

saffron
bracelet

Crocheted beads can sometimes be found online and in craft stores, but you can always make your own. While crochet pieces can look homely, the combination of metallic spacer beads and vibrant colours makes this chic bracelet anything but. Perfect to jazz up everyday jeans and sweater, it would also look stunning against a little black dress in the evening.

Materials

Makes a 19cm (7½in) bracelet

Wire cutters

Flexible beading wire, medium

Crimp beads

Crimping pliers

Beads:

    12 x 3mm faceted metal beads, or more if you need a larger bracelet (Bead A)

    8 x 8mm bead caps (Bead B)

    4 x 17mm crocheted beads, ready-made or made following instructions on page 106 (Bead C)

    4 x 18mm metal spacer or round beads if spacers aren't available (Bead D)

Beading awl

2 jump rings

Toggle set with 18mm ring and 20mm bar

1 Cut a 30.5cm (12in) length of flexible beading wire. String on a crimp bead, and pass the end of the wire back through the bead, forming a small loop. Crimp the bead and trim the excess wire.

2 Put three Bead A onto the wire, followed by a bead cap (Bead B) facing upwards. Then string on a Bead C, a Bead B facing downwards and a Bead A. Next, string on a Bead D.

3 Continue stringing on the beads in the same sequence: A, B, C, B, A, D, until you come to the last crocheted bead. Put on a Bead D, followed by three Bead A and a crimp bead. String the end of the wire through the crimp bead, and through the last faceted bead you strung. To help with tension, put a beading awl through the loop and pull the beading wire tautly. Crimp the crimp bead and trim the excess wire.

4 Attach jump rings to the loops of the wire, and then attach each jump ring to each part of the clasp to finish the bracelet.

Spaced Out

Since wrist sizes vary, you can vary the diameter of the larger spacer beads, as well as the number of small faceted beads, to lengthen or shorten the bracelet.

advanced
★★★

midsummer earrings

Crocheting with glass beads turns an ordinary set of metal hoops into a summery treat. Use a fine crochet hook, perle cotton and nimble fingers for this advanced crochet project. If you want to take this a step further, you could always crochet a little bag or scarf to match.

Materials

25–30 small, light blue, glass beads

1 hank perle cotton #5, turquoise

Size 1 (2.00mm) steel crochet hook

1 pair of simple hoop earrings about 4.5cm (1¾in) in diameter

Key:

ch = chain stitch

sc = single crochet

st = stitch

Note: To prevent tangles in the thread, wind the hanks into balls before beginning.

1 To begin, string all of the beads onto your ball of perle cotton. It is not necessary to have the exact number of beads strung before beginning; however, it is better to have too many than too few beads strung. As you work you will need to slide the beads away from the hook as you go.

2 Make a slip knot and insert the crochet hook. Getting the first stitch around the hoop earring is the trickiest part. Grasp the tail of the thread and the hoop earring between thumb and middle finger of your left hand. With the thread forward, pass the hook through the centre of the hoop earring and behind, wrap a loop around the hook and bring the hook back through the earring to the front. Now there should be two loops on the hook. Grab a third loop and pull it through both loops.

3 *Insert the hook into the earring as before and wrap a loop around the hook and pull it back through the earring. Wrap a third loop around the hook and pull it through both loops on the hook. Repeat from * until the earring is covered all the way around. Next, ch 1, and turn the work. You are now ready to begin the lace pattern.

4 **Row 1:** Sc in next 3 st. *ch 2, pull one bead up close to the hook. Make the next ch, capturing the bead within the stitch. Ch 2, skip 2 st, sc in next 3 st. Repeat from * to the end. Ch 1, turn work. **Row 2:** Make 7 sc in each loop, to the end. In order to distribute the sc evenly in the loop, make 2 sc in first half of loop, 3 sc in the stitch that contains the bead, 2 sc in last half of loop.

5 Break the thread and weave in the loose ends. Repeat Steps 2–4 for the other earring.

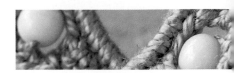

advanced techniques

This book only begins to cover what you can do when you learn to make jewellery. A large part of jewellery making involves casting, soldering, stone setting and more. These techniques can be learned from classes, as well as by studying books on metalsmithing. Here, I'll introduce you to a few of the more advanced techniques so that you can make your own findings and construct beautiful jewellery with precious metals and gemstones.

Making your own French wire (gimp)

Since most French wire (or gimp) is only widely available in base metal, I make my own using precious metals such as gold and pure silver. I use a quilt pin for this, although any long pin or needle will work well. Use about 23cm (9in) for enough gimp to make closures for one necklace.

You will need:

Bent chain-nose pliers
Straight pin
23cm (9in) length of 30 gauge precious metal wire, such as carat gold, sterling silver or fine silver
Wire cutters

1 Winding the wire

Using a pair of bent chain-nose pliers, grasp the pin and wire together just below the head of the pin. Position the jaw of the pliers so that it curves towards the head of the pin. Carefully begin winding the wire around the pin, creating a light coil. Keep the wire you are winding perpendicular to the pin as you wind around. If the coil is loose, use your fingernails to nudge the wire towards the head of the pin. After you have a bit of wire coiled, you can use your fingers instead of the pliers to hold the wire on the pin as you wrap.

2 Cutting the wire

When you have wrapped the wire as far as you can take it, remove it from the pin and cut it in half. You should have about 2cm (¾in) of wire when you are finished, before cutting.

Making findings with a torch

Making balled head pins and ear wires is a great way to experience working with a torch. The head pins are ready to use after polishing.

You will need:
Small butane kitchen torch
Wire cutters
Cross-locking soldering tweezers
Sterling silver wire, hard tempered 18 gauge, 5cm (2in) piece for ear wires, 4cm (1½in) piece for head pins
Glass dish of water
Self-pickling flux or borax (plus cooking pot or flameproof glass dish)
Copper, plastic or wooden tongs
Jeweller's polishing flannel

In a Pickle

Mix a pickle solution of 2 tbsp citric acid or alum powder to 225ml (8fl oz) hot water in a heavy-based cooking pot or glass container. Turn the heat to a low setting. Using tongs, dip the cut wire into the flux solution. When doing a batch of balled pins, it will be easier to pour flux into a small dish, and let the cut pieces of wire sit in the solution as you put a piece of wire into the flame.

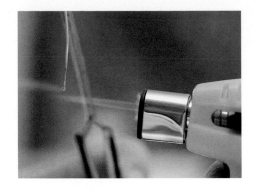

1 Soldering
Turn the flame level to low on the torch, ignite the torch and press the lever that will keep the flame on automatically. With your soldering tweezers, take a piece of wire and hold the end of the wire in the blue flame, perpendicular to the direction of the flame.

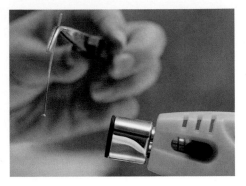

2 Balling up
The wire will turn red and start to ball up. As soon as the ball starts to form to a diameter of about 1mm, remove from the flame.

3 Pickling
Still holding the wire with your tweezers, dip the wire into the dish of water, and then drop it into the pickle solution.

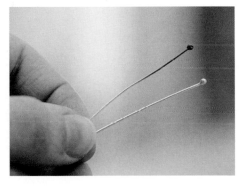

4 Polishing
Leave in the pickle solution for at least half an hour, or until the wire has a whitish coating. This white coating is a layer of pure silver. Polishing with a jeweller's cloth will usually remove this layer.

advanced
★★★

gemstone dangle

Multi-coloured sapphires could be used here if you have them, but high-quality cubic zircon beads give the same look at a fraction of the cost. A wire frame for the gemstone beads to rest on is made by flattening a piece of wire with a hammer.

Materials

Wire:
  2 x 10cm (4in) lengths of
  22 gauge sterling wire
  2 x 20.5cm (8in) lengths of
  28 gauge sterling wire
  2 x 8cm (3in) lengths of
  26 gauge sterling wire
Steel block
Chasing hammer
Round-nose pliers
Chain-nose pliers
Wire cutters
Beads:
  24–30 x 2.5mm faceted
  gemstone beads (Bead A)
  in assorted colours
  2 x 8mm gemstone
  briolettes (Bead B)
Pair of ear wires

1   Lay a piece of 22 gauge wire on the
    steel block. Hold the hammer at the
end of the handle, which will allow the head
to do most of the work with gravity. Hold the
piece of wire on the steel block with your
fingers off to the side of the wire. Gently tap
the wire with the flat face of your hammer,
flattening a length of about 4.5cm (1¾in) in
the middle of the wire, so that the middle
section becomes fairly flat and measures
about 1mm across. Repeat for the other
piece of 22 gauge wire. Create a closed
wire-wrapped loop on both ends of the wire
(see page 50).

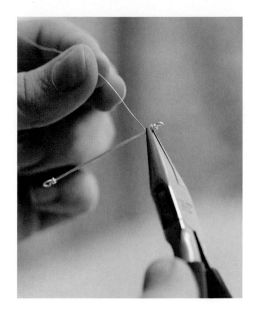

2 Take a 20.5cm (8in) length of 28 gauge wire, and hold the wire 2cm (¾in) from the end, perpendicular to the flattened wire piece, right next to the loop, using the round-nose pliers. Hold the wires together, and wind the long side of the wire around the flat wire three times. Wind the short end of the wire around the coil of your wire-wrapped loop, and use your chain-nose pliers to press the end of the wire flush with the coil of the wire-wrapped loop.

3 Holding the loop, slide one Bead A onto the 28 gauge wire, so that it sits on the flat piece of wire. Hold the bead and wind the wire around the flat piece four times. Continue stringing between 12 and 15 Bead A on the wire. Wrap 2cm (¾in) of the remaining 28 gauge wire around the coil of the wire-wrapped loop.

4 Attach an ear wire to the other loop of the stick. Make a briolette wrap on a Bead B with 26 gauge wire (see page 54), and attach to a loop on the end of the gemstone-wrapped stick. Repeat Steps 2–5 for the second earring.

Flat Out

As you practise hammering, note you can adjust the width of the flattened wire by modifying the amount of times you strike, as well as the force behind the strikes.

advanced
★★★

lunar necklace

A moonlike glow from the chalcedony and fire opal beads complement each other for an ethereal, delicate gemstone necklace in sterling silver. By simply hammering the connecting jump rings, the textured surface will catch the light and add to the shimmering effect of precious metals and gems.

Materials

**Makes a 33cm (13in)
  necklace**

Ball peen hammer and steel
  block
1 x 8mm jump ring
Beads:
  1 x 8mm chalcedony
  briolette
  9 x 3mm fire opal rondelles
  (Bead A)
  8 x 2.5mm chalcedony
  rondelles (Bead B)
4 head pins
Round-nose pliers
Bent chain-nose pliers
Chain-nose pliers
Wire cutters
1 x 3mm jump ring
2 x 5mm jump rings
30.5cm (12in) length of 24 or
  26 gauge silver wire
33cm (13in) length of fine
  sterling silver chain
Clasp and jump ring set

1 On your steel block, lightly strike the 8mm jump ring, using the round end of the hammer's head. Don't hit too hard to flatten the wire, you want to achieve a consistent texture. When you have the hammered finish that you want, stop, as it is easy to overwork the surface.

2 Using a briolette wrap (see page 54), wrap the chalcedony briolette to the hammered ring. Follow with wrapping a fire opal on a head pin, on each side of the briolette.

3 Cut a 4cm (1½in) piece of wire, and make a wire-wrapped loop onto the hammered ring. Add Beads B, A, B, and attach to the 3mm jump ring with a wire-wrapped loop. Carefully rotate the loop so that the jump rings are perpendicular to each other.

4 Hammer the two 5mm jump rings on the steel block. Make a closed wire-wrapped loop on one of the jump rings with a piece of 24 gauge wire measuring 4cm (1½in) long. Slide on beads B, A, B. Make a wire-wrapped loop, attach to a piece of 2cm (¾in) chain, and wire wrapped closed.

5 Thread the chain by the other end through the jump ring holding the pendant. Attach a 5cm (2in) piece of wire to the end of the chain, and slide on Beads B, A, B. Attach to the hammered jump ring with a wire-wrapped loop.

6 Cut two more 4cm (1½in) lengths of wire, and attach Beads B, A, B as before, making a loop and attaching it to a jump ring. Make a loop and attach each side to a 16.5cm (6½in) length of chain. Cut two pieces of wire measuring 2.5cm (1in) each. Attach to each end of the chain. Put a fire opal bead on each wire, and wire wrap to the jump ring and clasp.

baroque pearl bracelet

Baroque freshwater pearls come in an organic shape and style that is quite different from the perfect sphere pearl we are all used to seeing. Gold spacers and red silk thread make a simple knotted bracelet exotic.

Materials

Makes a 19.5cm (7¾in) bracelet

Silk beading thread, size E

12 x 10mm baroque pearls

13 x 4mm vermeil or high carat gold spacers

2cm (¾in) French wire, cut into two pieces

J-hook clasp and jump ring

Wire cutters

Beading awl

G-S Hypo Cement or strong glue

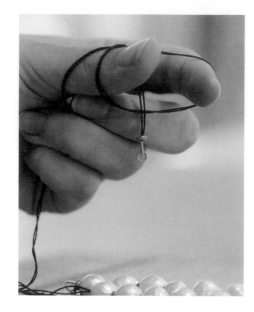

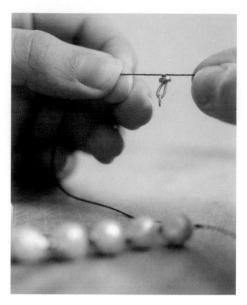

1 Follow Steps 1–5 of Classic bead stringing (pages 22–23), alternating the gold beads and pearls and using a 10mm piece of French wire. Start and end with a gold bead followed by the clasp. Slide the first bead onto the French wire loop. Hang the bead along with the clasped end over your index finger and thumb. Use your ring and middle finger to hold the rest of the bead below the thread in the crease of your finger, which will help maintain the best tension. Loop the bead back over your thumb, and cross over the thread with the bead dangling in the middle of the loop.

2 Lay down the strand, and put the tip of your awl in the centre of the loop (the start of an overhand knot). With your other hand, pull the longer part of the strand, closing up the knot. This will pull the first bead to the awl. Slide the bead down the awl by simultaneously pulling the long part of the thread. Use the fingernail of your index finger above the knot to push down. When you come to the surface of your beading mat, release the awl while still maintaining pressure with your fingernail.

3 Separate the two pieces of thread below the knot, tightening it. Slide down the next bead and repeat. Continue sliding and knotting the beads, until you come to the second to the last bead.

4 Release the slip knot, and pull the clasp tightly towards the knotted strand. Make a half hitch knot.

5 Make an overhand knot using your awl to tighten the knot. Dot G-S Hypo Cement or glue on the knot, wait a few minutes and then trim the thread.

advanced
★★★

jaipur jewels

Jaipur has long been a stone-cutting centre in India, and many gemstone beads purchased today still come from this region. Tourmaline comes in nearly all the colours of the rainbow, and I have chosen small faceted ovals in pink and blue for this project, together with Keishi pearls, a type of irregular pearl produced by oysters. Make your own ear wires from sterling silver wire to enhance the quality of the finished piece.

Materials

2 x 5cm (2in) lengths of
  prepared silver wire (see
  page 131)
Round-nose pliers
Pen or craft blade
Wire cutters
Needle file or sandpaper
54.5cm (21½in) length of
  28 gauge silver wire
20.5cm (8in) length of
  26 gauge sterling silver
  wire, cut in half
6 head pins
2 x 4mm jump rings
2 x 2mm faceted silver beads
2 x Keishi pearls
2 x pink tourmaline faceted
  ovals
2 x blue tourmaline faceted
  ovals

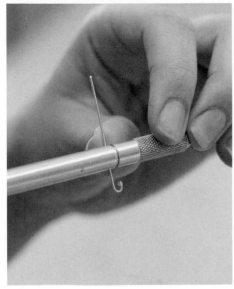

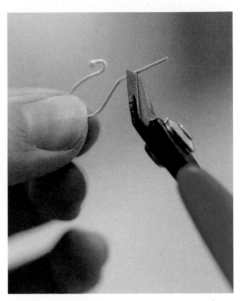

1 Start by making the ear wires. Use a prepared length of wire (see page 131). With your round-nose pliers, bend the wire just above the ball to form a U-shape. Use a pen barrel or craft blade barrel, and hold the looped end of the wire steady against the barrel with your thumb. With the other hand, wind the wire around the barrel, meeting the U-shape.

2 Remove the wire from the barrel, and bend the U-shape so that it is parallel to the rest of the wire. Use your round-nose pliers to make a slight upwards curve at the ball end of the wire.

3 Cut the wire to the desired length with wire cutters and then file the ends with a needle file or sandpaper until smooth.

Ear Wire Expertise

Hand-formed ear wires are available to purchase from retailers, but can be costly. By making your own, you not only save money, but have greater control of shapes and materials. Start out by making them in copper before you move on to more expensive metals, since it takes practice to get a consistent shape. I like to make several at a time, and then match the pairs after all are made. Use different implements such as marker pens or pens of varying widths, dowels and craft knifes to play with sizes. In addition to the balled version shown, you can experiment with a wire-wrapped version. Start with the same length of wire, but instead of the balled end, make a wire-wrapped loop end.

 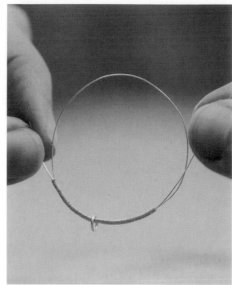 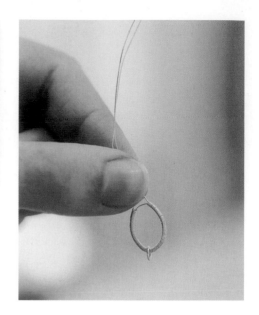

4 Make two pieces of handmade sterling or pure silver French wire measuring 4cm (1½in) each (see page 130). Make sure that the pin used to make the French wire is of a big enough diameter so that the inner diameter of the finished French wire will be large enough to accommodate two passes of the 26 gauge wire.

5 Slip one piece of French wire onto a length of the 26 gauge sterling wire. Then, slip a jump ring onto this wire. Slide both the French wire and jump ring to about 4cm (1½in) from one end.

6 Take the longer portion of 26 gauge wire and run it back though the section of French wire, creating a loop that holds the jump ring. Pinch the wire lightly from the top, to take up slack and form a teardrop shape.

Teardrop Shaper

If the teardrop shape doesn't form automatically, or looks 'off', you can adjust it by inserting a pen into the hollow of the teardrop frame to round out the bottom of the shape. Pinch the top of the teardrop to help create a point.

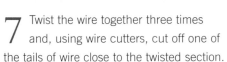

7 Twist the wire together three times and, using wire cutters, cut off one of the tails of wire close to the twisted section.

8 Slide on a silver faceted bead and make a closed wire-wrapped loop (see page 50). Make sure the loop is big enough to hang freely. Wire wrap a Keishi pearl and hang from a jump ring. Next, wire wrap a pink and blue tourmaline bead and put one on either side of the pearl.

9 Follow Steps 1–8 for the second earring. When you hang the teardrop from the ear wires, hang it so that the tourmaline beads are positioned symmetrically on each earring.

green garnet drops

Garnets come in a wide range of colours that you may not have seen before, such as the spring green used in this project. If you have trouble locating this stone, peridot stands in nicely, and is widely available. These earrings can also be made with gold-filled wire, using vermeil faceted beads to stand in for the 18ct faceted beads shown.

Materials

Beads:
  8 x 1.5mm faceted
  18ct gold beads
  2 x 6mm faceted green
  garden briolette
  2 x 3mm apatite rondelles
25.5cm (10in) 26 gauge
  18ct gold wire
4 x 18ct gold head pins
Wire cutters
Small 18ct curb chain, cut
  into two sections of three
  links, and into four
  individual links
Pliers
Pair of ear wires

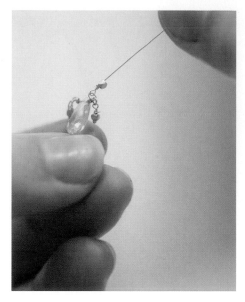

1 Wire wrap one 18ct gold bead onto each head pin and close the loops. Then wire the briolette. Cut the gold wire into a piece measuring 5mm (¼in). Thread the wire through the briolette, so that the briolette sits in the middle of the wire. Create a wire-wrapped loop and slip on an individual gold link, and then a head pin holding a faceted bead. Close the loop and repeat for the other side of the briolette.

2 Next, make a wire-wrapped loop, and hook to one of the individual links that are attached to the briolette wire. Close the loop, slide on a faceted gold bead, and create an open loop above this bead.

3 Attach the loop to an end link of one of your three link chain sections. Repeat for the other side of the briolette.

4 Wire wrap an apatite bead, closing the loop that will hang from the ear wire, leaving the other loop open. Hook this loop onto the middle link of the three link chain that is attached to the briolette, and then close and wrap the loop.

5 Attach the earring to an ear wire by the apatite bead. Repeat Steps 1–5 for the second earring.

Glossary

briolette – a type of teardrop-shaped bead with holes drilled horizontally near the top of the bead. Usually faceted, these beads are made from glass and precious or semi-precious stones.

burnish – to smooth the surface of polymer clay by rubbing.

carat – a unit of measurement that describes the amount of pure gold in an alloy of gold.

clay extruder – a metal tube that foces polymer clay through an interchangeable disc. Makes uniform coils of ribbon and tiles from clay.

conditioning – the action of kneading and working polymer clay to make it pliable.

crimp – to squeeze metal together in order to create ridges. Crimping with a pair of crimp pliers and a crimp bead will create a secure ending on a string of beads.

faceted – a stone or bead with a cut surface.

felting – to create a sturdy fabric by causing wool fibres to mat together with a needle or with water.

findings – small items such as clasps, jump rings and ear wires that are components in creating jewellery pieces.

firescale – a dark coating of cuprous oxide that forms on metals containing copper when exposed to high flame.

firing – the process of baking ceramics, such as polymer clay pieces in the oven.

flux – a solution containing boric acid, which is necessary in soldering to create a clean join. It can also be used to protect silver from firescale when heating.

french wire – a coil of very fine gauge wire. Also known as gimp or boullion.

gauge – a term of measurement, used to size beads, metal wire and sheets. Also, a tool to measure beads, wire and sheets.

hammered – a finish with a dimpled look that is applied by striking metal with a hammer.

head pin – a piece of wire, usually under 5cm (2in), with a ball or head at one end, used to hold a bead.

jump ring – a small ring, usually under 1cm (½in). It is used as a finding to connect beads, wire, chain or even other jump rings in creating jewellery.

mandrel – a cylinder-shaped tool used for forming metal rings or bracelets.

precious metal – metals that have a substantial monetary

value and can be traded, such as silver, gold and platinum.

rondelle – a saucer-shaped bead that is often faceted.

semi-precious – a gemstone that has some value, yet is not as valuable as a diamond, ruby or sapphire.

solder – a mixture of precious metal with lesser metal that has a lower melting point than the precious metal. It is used in *soldering*.

soldering – the action of joining metal along a seam or two pieces of metal together.

temper – the degree of hardness or elasticity of a metal. A tempered metal has been strengthened by heating or by manipulation.

wool tops – lengths of wool fibres that are used for felting.

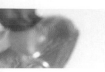

Resources

SHOPPING RESOURCES

These suppliers carry everything you need to make the projects in this book from wool tops, beads and findings.

ACTACROWN LIMITED
Suite 6, 88–90 Hatton Garden
London EC1N 8PN
44 (0)20 7404 1110
Fine quality gemstone beads and high carat gold beads and findings.

BEADWORKS
www.beadworks.com
Fine beads and beading supplies.

BLOOMING FELT
www.bloomingfelt.co.uk
Supplier of ready-made felted balls and feltmaking supplies.

COOKSON GOLD
www.cooksongold.com
UK supplier of precious metal wire, gemstones, chain and small torches.

ETSY
www.etsy.com
A website featuring thousands of individual shops selling beads, findings and other supplies. A great place for vintage beads and charms. Also has a techniques forum covering a wide range of jewellery-related topics.

JULESGEMS
www.julesgems.com
UK supplier with a wide range of beads, wire and other beading materials.

LAND OF ODDS
www.landofodds.com
Czech beads, delica beads, findings and tools.

MARYJANE'S ATTIC
www.maryjanesattic.net
Source of felting supplies: wool tops, felting needles and tools.

METALLIFEROUS
www.metalliferous.com
34 West 46th Street
New York, NY 10036
(212) 944-0909
A great source for wire, chain, tools and findings.

POLYMER CLAY PIT LTD
www.polymerclaypit.co.uk
UK supplier with a large assortment of polymer clay and tools.

PURL
www.purlsoho.com
Wide variety of fine cotton fabrics, yarns and notions.

REPRO DEPOT FABRICS
www.reprodepot.com
Fabrics and notions, with a focus on lightweight cotton reproduction prints.

SUNSHINE DISCOUNT CRAFTS
www.sunshinecrafts.com
Polymer clay and tools.

THE BEAD SHOP
www.beadshop.co.uk
21a Tower Street, Covent Garden,
London WC2H 9NS
44 (0) 20 7240 0931
Fine beads and beading supplies.

LEARNING RESOURCES

ABOUT.COM
www.jewelrymaking.about.com
Extensive jewellery-making instruction,
tips and resources.

CRAFTSTER
www.craftster.org
Online crafting forums with a dedicated
jewellery-making section.

GETCRAFTY.COM
www.getcrafty.com
Crafting community website with how-
tos, forums and more.

GLASS ATTIC
www.glassallic.com
Encyclopedia of all things polymer clay.
Tips, techniques, product reviews and
resources are covered in detail.

THE BEAD SOCIETY OF GREAT BRITAIN
www.beadsociety.org.uk
Non-profit organisation dedicated to
bead appreciation and jewellery
making. Contact Stefany Tomalin for
private stringing instruction.

Index

ACKNOWLEDGEMENTS

I'd like to thank my mother, Nancy Helt, for her support and also for her love of crafting, which she has passed down to me by fine example. I'd also like to thank Chris Sittel for his patience, encouragement and advice with design decisions. Thanks to Eva Gaskin, for her crochet expertise, the Log Cabin Quilters for their tips and assistance, and Stefany Tomalin, for her inspirational jewellery-making titles. A very special thanks to Sarah Rock, Holly Jolliffe, Mark Winwood, Gemma Wilson, Nel Hayes and Caroline King for producing beautiful photos, and Katie Hardwicke for her editing talents. Lastly, thank you to Michelle Lo and Miriam Hyslop for helping to make this book happen.

PICTURE CREDITS

Project photography by Holly Jolliffe
Step-by-step photography by Mark Winwood